Altogether Different

A memoir by
Brianna Wheeler

Korza Books
www.KorzaBooks.com
1819 SW 5th Ave #293
Portland, Oregon 97201

Cover Collage by Tareva Davis
Cover Design by Martin Eggiman Jr.
Interior Illustrations by Brianna Wheeler
Interior Layout and Design by Michael Schepps

First Edition October 2023
ISBN: 978-1-957024-05-9
Distributed and printed by Ingram
Korza Books name and logo are registered trademarks of Korza
Books LLC

For Grandma

Contents

San Pedro

The Peaches 'n Cream Barbie was released in the spring of 1985.

   Unlike Barbies of the preceding era that flirted with career aspirations like a flight attendant, doctor, ballerina, figure skater, or Malibu debutante, Peaches 'n Cream was something else entirely – more like the exclusive holiday dolls that were released each season. She arrived in an ethereal peach chiffon gown, rather than over-the-top-trendy femme separates. Her waxy yellow blond hair was curled and fluffed into a half-up half-down style, while her bright blue eyes were accented by a sheer wash of violet eyeshadow and the slim lips of her open-mouth smile blushed a shade pinker than the rest of her milky frame. The iridescent bodice of her gown sparkled like starlight and her skirt pouf-ed from her cinched waist in peachy, gossamer waves, accentuated by a dramatic peach chiffon stole and a single plastic diamond solitaire that hung from her freaky-long neck.

Like most six-year-olds with still-developing high-femme sensibilities, I needed this doll in my life.

And so on October 13, the Saturday after my seventh birthday, several schoolmates, church friends, and assorted cousins pre-gamed their Halloween costumes in my grandmother's backyard in celebration of my arrival on earth. I sometimes think my mother wanted an October child so she could throw costume parties every year. She was an excellent seamstress, designer, builder and artist, and when offered the opportunity to revel in those qualities, by, say, throwing a pre-Halloween birthday party for a dozen wide-eyed second graders, she shone her brightest.

It was during this annual costume party, when all our guests' masks had been pushed up over their foreheads and everyone held a second or third chunk of the sheet cake my mother decorated to match my Wonder Woman costume, that Peaches 'n Cream finally came into my life. When it was time to open gifts, all the costumed children, parents, cousins, aunts and uncles gathered around the piano in my grandmother's living room. She sat on the bench. I sat at her feet.

After I'd gracefully opened several gifts, sometimes folding the wrapping paper so as to not make too much mess, I was handed that familiar rectangular box, with the unmistakable weight, balance, and soft echo of a Barbie doll gently bouncing against thin

2

cardboard. I tore through the wrapping paper with much less charm than I'd approached the rest of my gifts.

The box did indeed contain the Peaches 'n Cream Barbie, but her mouth was pursed in a kind of ambivalent grimace, her ice-blue eyes were instead deep chocolate brown, her elegant violet eyeshadow was instead a trashy pale blue, and her jaw was square and wide. Her dress, shoes, and jewels were as expected, but the rest of her left me deeply dissatisfied. I held her in her unopened box and stared at her face in silence.

The party's host was my grandmother, whose modest, two-story suburban house was a cornerstone of my comfortable childhood, whose foresight had already begun aggregating investment accounts to ensure a comfortable future for her family, whose myriad talents had filtered through generations of ancestors to land in my hands and steer my entire life. She squawked with laughter and joked, "Now look, now look! Now she's too happy to speak," implying to our guests that I had rendered my otherwise overstimulated self catatonic with joy.

Her face quickly turned when I raised my eyes to meet hers, like she knew from my expression what was about to come out of my mouth. I lifted the Barbie up so the window into the box was visible to everyone, and, with feigned enthusiasm, sighed, "Oh, she's Black."

Two months later, I would spend the Christmas holiday with my father's family. And my paternal grandmother would gift me a white Peaches 'n Cream Barbie that I would love for several years.

This is my earliest recollection of a biracial experience.

Thirty-some years later and I still cringe at the memory of my underwhelmed reaction to receiving a Black Barbie, only to overstimulate myself with joy upon receiving the pale pink version. I wince when I think about how it must have made my Black mother feel, on the Christmas that I received the white Barbie, to watch her mixed daughter revel in her whiteness to the exclusion of her Blackness, while sitting in a room full of white people who were, in their own ways, still clumsily navigating the inclusion of Blackness into their own family. A family that, to their knowledge, had never been anything but white.

That I was in possession of both whiteness and Blackness wasn't a lesson I would learn for a decade. That I was in possession of two Barbies, one of which I found far more valuable than the other, however, was a lesson I absorbed immediately.

At age 42, all these peach-chiffon Barbie memories broke the surface tension of the emotions I'd been tamping down the pipe of my existence – the way a clogged drain will eventually flood a sink, then a bathroom, then a house, then the world. All because a drag queen named Trixie Mattel made an online video about their Barbie collection.

In 2020, the day the video was released, I watched it from the corner of my kitchen, where I sat at a black Ikea desk I bought for 20 bucks off Craigslist two years ago when I got tired of working from the kitchen table. When I sat at my desk, my back was turned to the entire house and I could lose myself in YouTube lethargy when I wasn't tossing blog posts into the void of the internet for increasingly smaller paychecks.

The shine of being a writer had worn off. I had only recently graduated from writing blogs for a frozen yogurt shop, a stamp maker, and a bird deterrent company that put high-pitched whistles on farms to scare away crows, to writing cannabis reviews for niche marketing websites and the event calendar for a free regional parenting magazine. Some teams that employed me paid me infrequently and, for others, the compensation dwindled even as the workload grew bigger. My work didn't feel important or even sustainable. And it certainly didn't feel like anything my grandmother would be proud of.

But at least I was a writer, right? Wasn't that a career to be proud of?

I hated thinking about it, so I hunched over my laptop, indifferent to the rest of the world, and leaned in as Trixie revealed the Peaches 'n Cream doll, a mint-condition model still in her original box. I felt like I'd been sucked backwards through a vortex.

The rush of emotions left me seasick. Suddenly I was a child, reliving the sight of my grandmother's face as I rejected a gift that represented so much more than any one Barbie doll should. In my mind's eye, I was seven-going-on-eight all over again, looking at my grandmother and rejecting my Blackness.

Everything is about a Black Barbie and nothing is about a Black Barbie. I remember so crisply the disappointment in my grandmother's eyes. The way her shimmery pink cheeks slowly fell from beneath her eyes as her smile faltered. The glittering gold rims of her oversized square bifocals reflecting fading afternoon light from the living room's picture window. The wash of pearly sand polish on long almond-shaped nails as her fingers moved up to cover her quickly evaporating grin. Her legs crossed at the ankles, knees together, posture stiff and upright. I remember the golden hour filtering through her hair. The sour feeling of rejection mixed with disappointment mixed with vanity. Don't let the guests know you're disappointed. Smile. Say thank you.

The last 15 years of my life snapped into sharp relief. I wasn't disappointed with my life because I was an unsuccessful writer. I was disappointed with my life because I had abandoned my heritage.

This was a lot of emotional processing sparked by what should have been a low-stakes mood-mollifying 12-minute YouTube video, but it didn't materialize from nothing. I'd been struggling with heightened feelings of ineptitude since the recent deaths of my mother and grandmother. An established financial trust, including my grandmother's home, had reignited familial resentments, and my appetite for an inheritance reinforced the feeling that I was a disappointment.

Other inheritors had been taking advantage of this estate for years, and I was spiteful because I felt like I was the only grandchild disinclined to rely on savings meant for all of us.

I never thought I'd struggle in adulthood as much as I was struggling – financially, emotionally, and functionally. My son had recently been diagnosed with autism. Every day my writing career felt more like an exercise in childish nonsense, and certainly not the type of career that could support a gutted family with specialized needs.

The cacophony of the unknown had become deafening, but in 2020, panic became normalized. While my social media feeds waterfalled with the laments of acquaintances who withered in quarantine, my life remained the same pattern of confused, distressed parenting, followed by deep dissociating at my desk in the corner of the kitchen. I wanted to advocate for every single marginalized community, but when faced with my own son's disability, I'd never felt more useless.

Outside my front door, Portland was steadily becoming unmanageable. The news of George Floyd's murder flooded the streets with protests which were met violently by the Portland police, whose department and union clubhouse I lived squarely between. I could hear screams, gunfire, and sirens from intersections only a block or two away. Tear gas in my neighborhood was so thick that one night I ended up with hives after ducking into my backyard to smoke a joint.

During those weeks, there was a small, shrill vibration that hummed above the manic noise in my head: the name of my grandmother's favorite ancestor, Dangerfield Newby. The man whose heroic death begat the Civil War. A Black man, from whom I had descended, who died so that Black America could live free.

Watching the Trixie Mattel video, what I'd maintained were superficial feelings around being biracial, about advocacy and activism, about art and power and family, all snapped into focus. My feelings of never quite belonging anywhere but also, with minimum assimilation, fitting in anywhere, filled me with sudden shame. I think I am a Black woman – I say I am – I want to be. But as a child, I was given the choice, and I chose whiteness.

I hadn't known before that I chose to be white. I hadn't realized that was a choice I could make. And I hadn't recognized that I spent every intervening year between that birthday and this moment further distancing myself from anything that would distinguish me as more than harmlessly beige. Different, but not too different.

The first time I was prescribed glasses, I put them on and thought, "What the fuck? Is this how everyone sees?" I was dumbfounded. I didn't know my vision was impaired until it was adjusted. Watching Trixie Mattel show off her Barbie evoked a similar response. It was like a wall came down and revealed a whole other forgotten room filled with feelings of regret and disappointment and failure that I only just realized was even there – but oh my god, now that I could see it, I knew so clearly it had been there the whole time. It was the loudest room, the biggest room, and it had been crowding everything else out while I let my attention wander elsewhere.

When my mother and I talked about feminism, she would roll her eyes over my contemporary takes, her lens crystalized by a movement from which she'd fallen by the wayside long before I was born. When she was making a point, or trying to sound bougie, she had this tendency to overemphasize the letter *W*. "A woman's right to work, harumph, we've always worked, Brianna – *hw*hite *hw*omen fought for that crap, not us. We always *hw*orked, we *hw*orked for them!" And I would roll my eyes back at her, aware that real intersectionality was a challenge, but unwilling to recognize how much. Always assuming her experience and mine were essentially the same, annoyed by her over-pronunciation.

Was I Black because my mother told me I was? Or was I as white as so many people assumed I was? Was I a good advocate because I was born from one, or was I just another armchair activist mining social capital from a Black mother who understood societal abandonment better than I ever would?

And, fuck, how disengaged must I be from any sense of heritage or purpose if I'm asking this of myself so late in the game?

****

For months I'd been ignoring a stack of genealogy research I'd taken from my grandmother's house after she died. I had the intent to sift through it and try to organize it into a timeline, but the stories I skimmed were terrifying, traumatic, and too complex to unpack, so they just sat on my bookcase, gathering dust.

But in watching Trixie Mattel wax about her pale white Peaches 'n Cream Barbie, watching her wind the chiffon stole around her fingers, and hearing her describe how she spent her childhood repressed, desperately longing for the heterosexual girlhood that she knew she couldn't have, I'd seen a flash of my own seven-year-old self and her desires.

Would she be as disappointed with the adult version of herself as I was?

For the first time since her death, I opened my grandmother's messy stack of research, looking for stories about Dangerfield Newby. I began organizing both her life's work and my own abrupt geyser of messy memories. A dam had burst, a wall had fallen, a bathtub had overflowed, and I was being swept away.

Or maybe I was swimming, I'm still not sure.

In 1993, San Pedro High School had a student body of about 2,500. A large percentage of students were Mexican (or Native, considering the city's 130-mile proximity to the Mexican border), but even the white population was largely composed of second- or third-generation Croatian or Italian immigrants. The racial ambiguity wrought from the mashup of so many cultural combinations made it easy for a biracial kid like me to integrate with ease.

Truly, I wasn't physically aware of my own Blackness, or any type of other-ness, until my sophomore year of high school. I was an enthusiastic contributor to the theater department, and in 1993, for the fourth time in a row, I was cast as a maid in a school theater production.

In prior years, even though I never seemed to land a leading role, I was usually cast in a substantial supporting role with at least one big solo number, which was always good enough for me. However, that year, all my parts somehow happened to be maids. I wasn't bothered by it; something about no small parts, only small actors. In the last play of the school year, I even got to flit around the stage in a French maid costume, a garter belt with fishnets, and shiny black stiletto heels, while twirling a feather duster. At 15 years old, I was more excited by how well I filled out the costume than offended by an implication.

The musical opened with me, alone in a parlor, dusting a bookshelf, slightly bent with my backside to the audience so they could see the straight lines of my stockings and the peek of ruby red underwear that was included in the costume-shop ensemble.

The crowd lit up with wolf whistles and hollers as soon as the curtain rose and illuminated my backside.

My grandmother finally saw the performance on closing night. She lodged a complaint with the school's drama department the next Monday. She was livid. Why were they repeatedly casting her Black granddaughter as a sexualized house servant?

I didn't understand why she was so mad. The audience loved me.

In 2006, my partner and I moved from California to Oregon, a state that, until 1926, forbade Black residency in its constitution. We didn't know that. We just liked the Northwest.

We moved into Portland's "historically Black" neighborhood, which struck me as bizarre. I could go days without seeing a white person when I was living in southern California, but I'd never heard anyone refer to an entire city section as a "Black" or "white" neighborhood. I was so removed from bias.

Portland's Black neighborhood, I would learn several years after we settled, is designated as such because when Oregon finally amended their constitution to allow Black residents, it was primarily so Black men could work at riverside shipyards. When their insular, Portland area community, a hastily built assortment of cheaply made homes constructed atop a floodplain, was inevitably washed away in the great Vanport Flood of 1948, the residents were relegated to the neighborhood I settled in or the neighborhood just north of mine, which, in turn, was razed between 1960 and 1970 to build a new hospital and freeway. The majority of those Black residents were displaced without adequate recompense, the city citing eminent domain.

When we settled here, we wondered how we'd landed such an affordable house with a yard, a driveway, and a picket fence in such a nice neighborhood. When locals from the other side of town referred to it as a ghetto, I'd snap that they'd obviously never seen a ghetto, images of Los Angeles' vast assortment of skid row tent cities burned into my brain. I should have demanded an explanation of what exactly made the neighborhood ghetto. I should have asked them what they thought a ghetto was. But I knew what they were referring to, and I should have snapped at them to stop being so fucking racist.

When my partner and I married four years later, we did so in the town of Estacada, a Mt. Hood logging village just outside of Portland. Estacada had not been historically memorialized as a "sundown town," but it most likely was. Most of Oregon was. And just because Estacada hasn't officially admitted to historically being a white-only community, that doesn't mean someone else's granddaughter isn't ignoring her own stack of inherited research to the contrary.

For the uninitiated, a sundown town is a town where it's illegal to be Black after sundown. A Black person is only allowed to pass through a sundown town during daylight hours; they may not own property in the town, or even stay within city limits once the sun has set. Sundown towns are white-only. Before Black people were admitted residency to work the shipyards, Portland was a sundown town too.

This rural area of Oregon is notoriously bigoted, but it would be years before I associated what I learned about sundown towns decades prior in an African-American history class with what I knew of the state I chose to settle down in.

Estacada, the town where we got married, was a former logging hub which sat at the foot of Mt. Hood. We chose it because of the Safari Club, an old trophy hunter lounge turned dive bar. It was also an event space with natural history style exhibits, featuring antique now-endangered game trophies like white tigers battling in the foreground of a hand-painted jungle diorama, and grazing gazelles on airbrushed African plains, and penguins floating on acrylic ice caps. A polar bear loomed over the club's entrance.

Though we rented almost all the rooms in the one local hotel, my family all traveled back to Portland after the reception to stay at the downtown Hilton. At the time, I wondered why. I wouldn't become aware of Oregon's history of hostility until several years after my wedding, during one of my mother's annual visits.

My mother and father actually lived in Salem, the capitol city of Oregon, for a short time. They met while working at a Montgomery Ward in San Diego, California, then moved to Salem for a corporate opportunity. I was born there, on the 45th parallel. My mother said we moved back to California when I was three because she was "tired of being the only Black woman in the whole city." She said it like it was the punchline to a joke, but there was a sharpness as well. I now hear this as a sanitized version of, "I feared for my safety and the safety of my biracial daughter in a city where no one looked like us and no one wanted to look at us."

She shared that memory with me as we cruised back into town after spending the day exploring Mt. Hood. Like it was an anecdote at a cocktail party. So casual. We were on the highway that led from the mountain back into the city, and in front of us a truck towed a flat bed strapped with two motorcycles. When we were close enough, we could see Nazi symbols (a swastika and a SS) on its rear fender, as well as the fuel tanks and the sidecar attached to the older-looking of the two bikes.

My mother loved the Northwest, and we agreed that the region was some kind of paradise. It took me so long to recognize how insidious the homogeneity of the region could be.

But I love it here. Even though, with each passing year, my skin fades another shade lighter than the peachy gold it was the year before. Even though so many people

I meet assume I'm white too, which, I take offense to correcting, because in those moments I almost always feel as if my Blackness is being snatched away by a stranger. Offense feels like an elemental response to something vital being stolen from me, like I'm responding to the theft of a possession I was not aware could be snatched away. I am offended to be mistaken for white.

I had very little experience correcting this faux pas before relocating to Oregon. It took several awkward, stilted interactions to develop the language I needed to gently correct someone and still avoid confrontations, even after my claim to Blackness was met with rejection ("no way! But you're not *Black* Black!"), tone-deaf compliments ("wow, how lucky you're so light!"), or a hamfisted attempt at connection ("oh, you're Black? I grew up in poverty, I totally get it"). In too many scenarios, someone would share a favorite n-word joke, told with a qualifier that their "one Black friend thinks this is so funny." Sometimes I roll my eyes and say nothing. Sometimes I don't even bother rolling my eyes. I know what it's like to be someone's one Black friend.

Living in Oregon brought me face to face with both the idea of disappearing into my whiteness, but also the knowledge that complete assimilation would never be successful. I would always be just different enough to raise eyebrows, no matter how blond the hair or how fair the skin. Since junior high I've colored my hair and worn loudly patterned clothes, calling attention to myself on my own terms, because it's been my experience that when people can't categorize you they're inclined to make assumptions, and when those assumptions don't line up with their expectations, well, sometimes their cluelessness leads to confrontation. And most of the time, that confrontation is not worth the effort.

In this home I've chosen, I must reckon with how many times I said nothing while a white friend or acquaintance I admired said or did something outright racist. How many times I could have stood up to ignorance and didn't. How many times I chose the lasting scar of someone else's ignorance over the brief discomfort of righteousness.

Even if I claim this behavior as some type of self-preservation, neither my mother or my grandmother had that privilege. I'm hiding under a thin blanket of assimilation that's long since worn through. These women raised me better than that. They raised me to stand up for what's right, to be unafraid to correct bigotry or racism. They raised me to be unapologetically Black.

Yet here I am in Portland, divorced from my heritage and whatever purpose it comes with. So divorced, in fact, that it was the resurgence of a dusty, all-but-evaporated 30-year-old memory of a Barbie doll that galvanized me into recognizing that I'd rejected my

Blackness at all. Yet even though I'd rejected it by choice, I sure was offended when someone assumed I didn't own it.

I'd wasted this gift of identity from my ancestors. Blackness was a gift that was won through years of suffering. My existence was a gift born from a struggle that I'm too privileged to ever truly wrap my brain around. So were these gifts wasted on me?

And who am I to think I won't waste the rest of their gifts?

****

For most of my childhood, my grandmother worked as a supermarket clerk. Hers was the most popular checkout lane, and she often came home on holidays with armfuls of gifts and cards from her customers. My oldest cousin loves to tell the story of my grandmother seeing a young Black man's job application in the trash can, retrieving it, and confronting her white boss about it. She stood her ground, kept her charm and cool, and convinced the boss he was acting in poor taste before ensuring the kid got his interview. That kid was hired and eventually became the store manager before being promoted to a corporate position.

I'd heard several stories from my grandmother about past generations, but she had never told me about the resume she rescued from the wastebasket. A resume that was rejected on sight, simply because the applicant was Black. I don't think she thought it was an example of exemplary behavior. She was doing what a lot of Black women do, and have always done, under circumstances and hardships that I can scarcely conceive – quietly caretaking her community, doing what she could when she could with what she had to make the next generation of Black people's lives, hopefully, better.

My mother was a teacher with the Los Angeles Unified School District for more than 20 years. During that time she was passed over for promotions yearly, despite the fact that her contributions to the art, drama, and history departments included vibrant street-facing murals, community arts and crafts festivals, and even therapy-based after school programs. In her spare time, she taught both children and adults how to draw mandalas at the local community college.

My mother became a legacy in our small town, an elementary school teacher who trafficked exclusively in low-income, working-class neighborhoods. Generations of children touched by her vivacious brilliance and tender validation now stop me on the street or in the supermarket whenever I visit San Pedro to share their warmest memories of my mother.

She would keep my class picture in her wallet, and whenever her feistier male students would act up, she would promise to show them a picture of the most beautiful girl in the world as soon as they calmed down. When they got their act together, she would flash them my current class picture. It must have worked; it was a gimmick she used for years.

I wonder what those students would say if they could see how in my maturity, I look more and more like my mother, albeit much lighter skinned.

After she retired, she taught other retirees how to create their own mandalas with low-cost workshops she organized at the nearby technical school. The mandalas, she explained, were both a way to process trauma and to access a kind of primordial creativity, which she maintained existed in all of us.

I wonder, how does an upbringing peppered with stories like this result in an adulthood devoid of the same feelings of obligation? Or is freedom from these obligations the whole point of my existence? If I'm not a brilliant Black woman exhausting herself in a struggle to make a better world for our people, or at least my own family – if I'm not keeping this altruistic torch of my mother's lit – then why am I here?

Are these burdens? Or is this legacy? Do I earn this mantle or inherit it? Or both?

Looking back at their lives, it's as if every act was performed in the service of bettering the commonwealth: my mother teaching in working-class neighborhoods, thousands of lives left richer for her having contributed herself to them; my grandmother, gathering scraps of family history – battered library books and letters, newspaper clippings, even cousins lost to time and found through internet genealogy sites. She braided them together so that her granddaughter's granddaughter's granddaughter could have the extraordinary gift of her own history. Doing what Black women do, making the next generation of Black people's lives, in this case, her own family, hopefully, better.

I was fortunate to learn at my mother's and grandmother's feet. If I don't use what they taught me, I am a failure.

There was so much I wanted to achieve before they died. There was so much to say that I could never bring myself to say. While my mother gasped her last breaths, I hunched in the corner of her hospital room typing up product descriptions for an Amazon seller to fulfill a freelance contract. The righteousness that she taught me, which I should have been employing to communicate for her, was instead being employed to snap back at the seller's insistence at including KitchenAid mixers and waist trainers in his Mother's Day gift guide.

In the weeks before my grandmother died, I was chasing deadlines, steamrolling my feelings in favor of writing essays about getting high, while a published record of this legacy's weight, a 276-page book titled *Migrants Against Slavery,* moldered in the corner of my musty bookshelf. The time to read it, and discuss it, and ask every question that I wanted to ask, was slipping away.

****

It was the summer of 2017 when my sister called with news of our grandmother's impending death.

I traveled from my home in Portland, Oregon back to San Pedro to assist with the end of life plans, support my cousin and sister who had provided our grandmother's palliative care, and attempt to connect with my grandmother as she approached what she referred to as "her reward." She called it this because her faith informed her she would reunite with all her loved ones in heaven.

A decade before her death, while we shopped for my wedding dress, she sat watching me twirl in a $80 prom dress my mother would later that week alter into something spectacularly bridal. She held a monogrammed handkerchief to her mouth and with a trembling sigh she said, "how lucky are we to see Brianna get married before I get my reward." Then she opened her pocketbook, retrieved a compact mirror and reapplied her raspberry lipstick, using the handkerchief to wipe away the pigment that escaped the borders of her mouth.

As my grandmother's death approached, this memory ricocheted back and forth between sorrowful and joyful with such ferocity I thought my eyes would cross. She said it herself. Death was her reward.

My mother had died three years prior, and the unchecked grief I had regarding her death had twisted my emotions around my grandmother's parting. During my stay, I bent over backwards to comfort the family, while doing very little to manage my own looming implosion. My feelings of helplessness were obscured with a fabricated zen competence I had developed to camouflage my vulnerability.

All I wanted to do was sob, but I sat beside my grandmother in silence as she commentated on her programs. Instead of revealing the depths of my emotion, I reflected her atmosphere the way a mirrored lake reflects a clear blue sky while hiding a thousand capsized rowboats.

My grandmother always relished her role as the family historian, but I admit, I often tuned out her sermons on our genealogy. It's not that I didn't recognize these stories as clandestine or appreciate their importance – it was the way my grandmother spun them that I didn't like.

She spoke often of her favorite ancestor, Dangerfield Newby, who died heroically in battle. He was the first freedom fighter killed at Harpers Ferry, an event that initiated a civil war which would end American slavery. Dangerfield was the oldest son of our original family matriarch, a woman who, to hear my grandmother tell it, had escaped slavery through the power of love by marrying a hero of a man, an immigrant, who freed her and all her children so that our family may blossom into what it is today.

My grandmother told these stories clumsily, juggling ages and timelines to suit her mood or audience. They were tales of tragedy told tenderly, and the awkward omissions and romanticized storylines made me cringe. A child bride reimagined as a capable young woman, a slave owner described as a hero for freeing his biracial children, a plantation master understood as kind and generous, but never as philandering.

However, in the weeks leading up to my grandmother's death, these stories she'd been telling us our whole lives suddenly meant everything to me. I wanted to re-learn them all.

It was while we passively watched *Gunsmoke* on basic cable that my grandmother asked me if I'd yet read *Migrants Against Slavery: Virginians and The Nation*, a book she'd been shoving into my hands for the last decade.

Written by historian Philip J. Schwarz and published in 2001 by the University of Virginia Press, *Migrants Against Slavery*'s central thesis is that the exodus of residents from Virginia to free states prior to the Civil War radically changed the national discourse on slavery – an exodus of which my own family was very much a part.

I remember when my grandmother found this book. It was on a trip to visit me in Portland. She had been researching the African-American history section of Powell's Books online in anticipation of her trip, and was so eager to collect all the books she'd found on our ancestry. I drove her and my grandfather to the west side entrance and spent the afternoon reading comics in the cafe while my grandfather napped in the passenger seat of their brand new Corolla.

The memory evaporated and I looked over at her. She was absorbed in the vintage Gunsmoke drama, nestled in a power recliner beside the couch. When she needed it, the chair would push her into a standing position so she could lean into her walker and shuffle herself to, as he referred to it, the commode. But now she had it reclined just slightly, her feet elevated, and her hospital socks peeking from underneath one of two knitted afghans. I asked if she wanted me to read aloud from her copy, and without breaking her focus from the television she said, "No. Just skip ahead and read chapter seven."

I opened it up and began thumbing through the pages. I wondered how my grandmother, whose literary taste orbited around Louis L'Amour exclusively, paced her reading. To me, this book smelled like school.

Chapter seven of *Migrants Against Slavery* is titled "The Newby Families in Virginia and Ohio." The Newbys are the point of origin for my matriarchal family story. It's momentous that our family has not only ancestors we can trace, but ones with enough historical significance to be written about several times over.

I should have been more excited about all the books my grandmother had found on that visit to Powell's. I looked at the worn price tag on *Migrants Against Slavery*'s back jacket and felt a pang of shame. I was ashamed at how disconnected I felt from all of this history. I was ashamed that it took her impending death for me to open this one simple book. But more than this, I was ashamed that in my hands, all this history might feel like it was all for nothing.

In the chapter's muddle of historical documentation, hearsay, and grandiose mythos, I found a portrait of a man, the only image in the chapter. An understanding of why my grandma had wanted me to connect with this story unfurled. This portrait was of Dangerfield Newby, who my grandmother spoke of fondly and often. In his face, I saw a reflection of myself. I saw an ancestor, but more than that, I saw an ancestor that looked like me.

This is a privilege not often afforded to biracial children.

Later that evening, I opened my sketchbook to a page hastily scribbled with messily paraphrased James Baldwin quotes I'd tried to note while watching the Raoul Peck documentary *I am not Your Negro* a few months prior. One broken interpretation stood out, but I could hear Baldwin's voice as I glossed over my shorthand, he was speaking about whiteness as a metaphor for power. "History is not the past. It is the present.... We are our history...the world is not white; it never was white, cannot be white. White is a metaphor for power."

Another note I gleaned from both the film and Baldwin's writing, I sketched a self portrait around. It was a reflection about the experience of whiteness and the experience of Blackness

"In this country,
For a dangerously long time,
There have been two levels of experience.
One can be summed up
In the images of Gary Cooper and Doris Day
Two of the most grotesque appeals
To innocence the world has ever seen.
And the other,

Subterranean, indispensable, and denied,
Can be summed up, let us say,
In the tone and in the face of Ray Charles:
> *Hey mama, don't you treat me wrong*
> *Come and love your daddy all night long*
> *All right, all is right now,*
> *I know it's alright, hey hey hey*
> *When you see me in misery*
> *Come on baby, see about me*

And there has never been any genuine
confrontation between those two levels of
experience"

But I was feeling that confrontation every day of
my life, whether I was aware or not. I was weary of
straddling a chasm, forever scrabbling to find purchase
against cliffs too sheer and barren to scale. I wanted to be
an invulnerable bridge over a fertile valley, built to
weather every storm until the end of time.

Reckoning with my grandmother's mortality, I
ached to disappear into Blackness. Whiteness was a
power I'd never learned how to wield.

That confrontation felt pretty fucking genuine.

and
there
has

never been any
genuine confrontation
between these two levels of
experience
~James Baldwin

Culpeper

At the foothills of the Blue Ridge Mountains, nestled into the northern tip of what was once the Confederate State of Virginia, is a small trio of adjoining counties: Culpeper, Orange, and Fauquier. The counties are marked by the rolling green hills that anchor them to the vast rural landscape. At the apex is a town called Culpeper, a small community that fades from its center into what feels like infinite farmlands.

Ribbony waterways massage the county borders, either linking or separating the constituencies, depending on your outlook. Crystalline lakes pepper the countryside, some with extravagant fountains, others more akin to a neighborhood swimming hole. The luxuries of this land appear suited to all types.

Each springtime, the banks of the Rappahannock, Rapidan, Hazel, and Thornton rivers erupt into dazzling wildflower displays. The small carmine petals of bloodflowers, whose deep red sap was used by Native tribes as an insect repelling sunblock, lazily float on the breeze like rusty snowflakes, easily swept away by even the softest breath. The rare yellow flowers sporadically produced by groundcovers of trout lilies, whose subterranean root networks span centuries, sway on long, tender stalks, their scarcity a bittersweet wonder. Bluebells, lady slippers, anemones and azaleas loudly radiate their Technicolor hues from corners, curbs, and groves, a luminous sea of roadside attractions, begging to be snatched, arranged, and lovingly placed on a windowsill.

In the fall, people travel from the farthest flung regions of the planet just to lay eyes on the trees in these counties. The foliage's annual transformation from fluttering greenery to brilliant, psychedelic chromaticity is a phenomenon so thrilling, it defines the region's tourism.

At the extremes, the winters are crisp but mild, tempered by the waterways and nearness to the Virginia shore, while the region's balmy summer temperatures rarely crest 90°.

This is all just to say, this land encompassing Culpeper, Fauquier, and Orange Counties, the land where my family lineage has been traced, is objectively and abundantly beautiful.

A little more than 150 miles east of Culpeper is Point Comfort, where in 1619, a ship carrying 20 enslaved Africans arrived on the colony's shore, heralding the start of the North Atlantic slave trade.

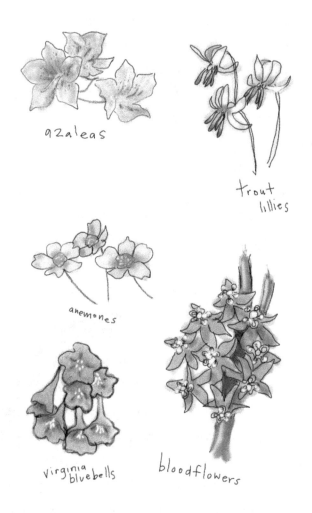

azaleas

trout
lillies

anemones

virginia
bluebells

bloodflowers

When learning about my family, Sam Fox was a point of origin. His name was prominent on the first page of my grandmother's messy notebooks full of aggregated history. He was a wealthy landowner, born and raised in Fauquier County, just north of Culpeper. His estate was substantial, and, in regards to slave labor, productive.

Because Sam Fox was born into a society that had established slavery as the status quo a hundred years prior, he never knew a world without slaves. Did Sam Fox ever have a moment of divine realization, or did he just live the same life day in and day out, blind to the atrocities of his everyday? I wonder, how did his moral compass inspire the behavior of his children? Was it with disgust or admiration that they carried on the Fox name?

I wonder this specifically because it was Sam Fox's youngest son, John, who history would consider the man who freed my family from bondage.

When Sam Fox died in 1804, he left his entire estate, including 16 enslaved men, women, and children, to his own scions, James, John, and Elizabeth Fox-Blackwell. Sam had a fourth, illegitimate child who wasn't formally included in the will, despite her numerous and aggressive objections after the fact. Her name was Dolly Ferguson.

Sam Fox's will stipulated that his daughter Elizabeth was to be the executrix of his estate, and that his slave inventory was to be passed down to his oldest son James.

AN EXCERPT FROM SAM FOX'S WILL
Reproduced in Sherrie Carter's
Who We Are: A Story of Strong and Lasting Roots of Black Fauquier County.
Self-published manuscript, 2001 edition. Typescript, p3

The script reads:

"Agreeable to an order of the Worshipfull court of Fauquier County, to us directed divide the estate agreeable to his will we have proceeded this twelfth of July in this year of our Lord, eighteen hundred and five."

James Fox's Part...	Black James
George - Blacksmith	Old Ovea
Ephraim	Alce
Peter	
Tatler	Two Feather Beds
Jalley	One Walnut Desk
Dilly and child	One Falling Leaf Table
Bob	One Pine Table
Fredrick	One Looking Glass
Benjamin	Bofatt & Sundries
Charity	Empty Case & Tea Board
Morgan	Smooth Bore Gunn
	Four Iron Pots, Two Dutch

A year after James inherited his father's Virginia estate, he was diagnosed as a "lunatik" and he died soon after. The Fox chattel of enslaved persons was then passed down again to the youngest Fox heir, John.

Sam Fox's estranged daughter Dolly was, once again, unincluded from the estate. Her chagrin was so great it became the defining story of her life – the story her children would tell for years after her death, as they watched the Fox estate grow more and more prosperous.

Over time, John Fox would become one of the wealthiest landowners in not just Fauquier County, but all of Virginia. According to a tattered page in one of my grandmother's two genealogy binders, John owned so much land and enslaved so many that his true inventory was a mystery. He was perceived as a stocky, morose bachelor who kept to himself, but perhaps what his neighbors saw was not the same as what the slaves he fathered saw.

John's wealth was established and maintained by "renting out" the Fox estate's enslaved laborers to job sites. The enslaved workers listed in John's "inventory" included blacksmiths, carpenters, farmers, cooks, hammermen, wetnurses, masons, wagoners, and laborers. Even management was delegated to slave labor; the enslaved were overseen by his groundskeeper, Eli Tackett, an enslaved Black man, who, in John Fox's records, is listed as "Mulatto."

The slave communities of Culpeper were complex networks spun throughout dozens of farms, businesses, and private residences where captives were leased. It was common for slaves within these networks to marry and parent children with slaves from other captors. Families would stretch between plantations and homesteads, husbands and wives miles apart. It was also common for the captive women to be raped by multiple masters.

There are so many shades of brown, but only one shade of white.

The lines between captor and captive never blurred, but the genetics blurred into an opaque spectrum that spanned deep mahogany to yellowy buttermilk. Personal histories were purposefully obscure; despite laws restricting relations between Black and white, biracial people comprised huge swaths of the enslaved community.

The things I've read about John Fox paint him, in between the lines, as a sympathetic slavemaster, and the oxymoron makes my eyes roll back so far they ache. I cannot comprehend this system. I can barely comprehend its wake.

**

Before Sam Fox perished and James Fox was committed, a woman owned by the Fox estate gave birth to a daughter she named Alce, which, in her stories a hundred years later, my grandmother would pronounce as EL-see. In letters between my grandmother and her cousin, the name appears as Ailsie, Alsie, and Asa. On Samuel Fox's inventory it's spelled Alce. In *Migrants Against*

Slavery, it's spelled Elsey. But I like the spelling Ailsie. It's so needlessly vowel heavy, I love it.

When Ailsie was five she became the property of John Fox. Any potential mother's story seems to unravel after the arrival of Ailsie, the only proof of her existence a bullet point on a slavemaster's last will and testament.

I imagine Ailsie's mother probably had rich, maple-syrup skin and a cottony-soft halo of sparkling ebony hair. I imagine she was long and lithe, graceful and demure, with sleek muscles defined by long days of work. I think she had a sugary sweet singing voice, like my grandmother's, and that she sang out loud and clear when working, but whispered soft when singing lullabies to her daughter. I imagine her child looked similar, a soft, round moon face with chubby cheeks and long eyelashes, a lighter skin tone. Perhaps Ailsie's rosy bronze skin was the culmination of her mother's deep hue and her unknown father's stark whiteness. I imagine this because until her 13th birthday, Ailsie worked exclusively in the main house of the Fox Estate, a job primarily reserved for the light-skinned enslaved.

Ailsie was a house servant. A light-skinned girl in a maid's costume.

I can only speculate on the details of Ailsie's and her mother's hair and skin and faces and bodies, but I enjoy imagining them looking a lot like my grandmother, their direct descendant who would be born in

40

neighboring Bridgeport, Ohio only 43 years after Ailsie's death.

Black Cowboys and Future Ancestors

Forty-three years.

Forty-three years doesn't seem like a lot of time to pass between my grandmother's birth and the death of our earliest known matriarch. After reading *Migrants Against Slavery*, this fact resonated so deeply within me that the vibrations made me nauseous; I was only a few generations removed from chattel slavery, and my mother and grandmother were barely removed at all.

Ancestors are a privilege, and for all the privileges my yellow skin affords me, I remain oppressed by the absence of my lineage past one or two generations. Who was Ailsie's mother? Who was Ailsie's father? Who was her great grandmother? As thrilling as it is to learn about her, I also feel the loss of all the history before Ailsie – history that, despite her work, I'm not sure my grandmother ever found.

After finishing chapter seven I wonder: How much history was ever available to find? How exhaustive has my grandmother's work been?

Grandma sits next to me watching black and white reruns on an HDTV, her oxygen tank humming, a crumpled tissue under the creased silk skin of her hand, her hair pulled into a coarse braid at the base of her neck and a knitted afghan around her shoulders. It occurs to me that I have no real understanding of ancestry. I only have her, and she's dying in a recliner next to me while she watches *Gunsmoke*.

She loves Westerns, but also the "idea" of the West. Black cowboys and sheriffs, mountains veined with gold, and, I imagine, the perceived absence of colonialism.   The wide open West represents a gateway to a burgeoning Hollywoodland, miles of palm tree-lined beaches blanketed with soft sands just waiting, even in the depths of wintertime, to caress the pale pink undersides of her delicate feet.

It makes me think that the West must have looked like the promised land to her when she was growing up in Ohio, where, beneath several feet of snow, Underground Railroad tunnels mapped a history whose expanse she'd never uncover in her lifetime.

When she was a child, I wonder, did she want to know that history or did she want to escape it?

Well, I wonder about those things now. Then, I buried my face in the chapter of the book she asked me to read, withdrawing from the present, avoiding her impending death. I really wish I would have taken the time, instead, to ask her all the questions about herself that I now ache to know. I wish I could have predicted how quickly the four months between this moment and her death would fly by.

Grandma's family came to San Pedro, California from Bridgeport, Ohio, because of her severe asthma, she said – the logic of which was explained to me many times, but still didn't quite stand up to scrutiny. Especially because she also told stories about how she and her sister would watch Klan gatherings from the window of the bedroom they shared. She described seeing burning crosses with a casualness I've only ever seen in Black grandmothers and great-grandmothers. Describing everyday horrors in everyday ways.

She held fast to her asthmatic origin story, but after hearing her detail the glow of burning crosses spilling through treelines to illuminate the bedroom of two little Black girls, I couldn't help but consider that my family's migration was a necessity for more reasons than my young grandmother's respiratory health.

But I get it. We tell the stories we tell for a reason, and who am I to reframe trauma that's already been reframed by the traumatized? For years, I ignored the history she tried to share because of the way she reframed that history. I considered her an unreliable narrator, but never considered myself to be an unreliable audience.

For so many years I just didn't care; now, nothing matters more.

****

The year I was born, my grandparents drove from their balmy suburban LA home to Salem to meet me. Every morning of their visit, my grandmother would sneak across the street to an empty lot that was replete with pear trees. I was born in the fall, and the pears were falling to the soft ground with ripeness. My grandmother would fill her arms with the fruits, messily gorging herself as she tiptoed back to our house.

She would tell this story like a giggly schoolgirl who got away with something. She would say that my grandfather chided her for stealing fruit, and recalls him warning her that neighbors would call the police if they saw her. I heard this as teasing, because of the wide smile my grandmother wore as she remembered it, but now I hear my grandfather's deliberate warning. I feel both thankful for my grandmother's version, that ripe pears are worth the hassle, and indignant over the truth of the danger in the story.

A few years into my Portland residency, one of my best friends came to visit. When I urged him to come with me on a walk through neighborhood back alleys to gather the ripe fruit that hung over the back fences, he cringed and held up his brown arm. "Not this Mexican. Girl, they will call the cops on me. I'm not trying to get shot."

****

My grandma had a copper complexion. My grandpa was a deep shade of chestnut. They had three children together: my mother, my uncle, and my aunt, approximately three-ish years each between them. They were the picture perfect Black American nuclear family. They were the representation their community needed, the first family of color to buy a home in tony West San Pedro.

My mother was the oldest, and her skin was the color of melted milk chocolate. My uncle was a forgettably ashy shade of oak. But the youngest child, my aunt, was born the shade of a buttermilk biscuit. It wasn't until my biracial self arrived some 25 years after my aunt's birth that the family was again blessed with this particular biscuit-y yellow hue.

My mother and her siblings would, throughout the course of their lives, go through periods of intimate closeness and violent contention. The ins and outs of their relationships remain a mystery; my mother is dead and my uncle is estranged. I'm sure my aunt's stories could fill in the gaps, but I avoid mining them; their turbulence turns my stomach.

The picture of my family that I held in my head for most of my life was one of beaming cinematic perfection. Since my mother and grandmother's deaths, stories that undermine that image have overtaken the Sears portrait ideal we projected through my childhood, so I rebuke them.

Before my mother's death, I asked her to live the last year of her life with me in Portland. I didn't know then that it was the last year of her life. 12 months after we first unpacked her suitcases, my sister, my grandmother and I sat in her cold hospital room as my mother took her last breath. My grandmother erupted like a volcano. She cried to Yahweh, "Take me instead! Please, take me!" She put her hands up to her face and sobbed the story of my mother's birth, a story that she retold so many times: how she looked at my mother's face when she was born and saw so much beauty and promise. "She was so *beautiful*," my grandmother wailed with heartbreaking emphasis. She cried when she brought her home and laid her down in the bassinet and she was so quiet and perfect, not like other babies. All of her friends' precious newborn babies simply could not compare to her beautiful first child.

My grandmother buried her face in her hands; over and over again she cried, "It should have been me." I looked up to the room full of white nurses and doctors and hated them for a million reasons I'll never be able to fully articulate.

I think my mother was the dream of my ancestors. She went to college and received advanced degrees. She graduated with honors, and went on to teach art, music and humanities to hundreds, if not thousands of families. She changed lives for the better, she uplifted those without the strength to uplift themselves, and she never stopped. Weeks before her death, she was having a meeting with the gay pastor of the multi-denominational church she'd just joined about teaching healing mandala art classes to the congregation. She was coming to Portland to die, and she still brought enough art supplies with her to teach a class of 30.

My mother was Black excellence, and I was excellent merely by my proximity to her. But she was far more complex than her facade, almost hypocritical to what she presented. When she died, I felt the excellence that I thought was armor fall away from me like wet cardboard, and what was left were inherited hypocrisies beneath. Maybe I hadn't inherited the best of her, and as my grandmother wailed, I feared that she was realizing the same thing.

In the weeks before my mother died, my husband and I planned a short, weekend camping trip. We excluded my mother from the planning, because I decided she was too compromised from rounds of radiation and the aftermath of a failed stem cell transplant to participate. I made that decision for her. Leaving her alone overnight felt risky, but not terribly so. She was still mobile, still clear headed, and still very much alive. When I came into her room to let her know we were heading out to the woods for an overnight camping trip, she brightened, and I realized she assumed she was coming as well.

I stammered something about how unsafe our style of primitive camping could be, how far we would be from any hospitals, how I wasn't even sure if there would be outhouses. She withered and even though I felt like I had broken her heart, I left her at home and went on the camping trip anyway.

The place we camped was near a waterfall whose ionic spray is said to have curative properties, Zigzag Falls. While we were on our overnight trip, instead of languishing on her deathbed, my mother scrubbed the entirety of our enormous sectional sofa. It was a monster of a couch we bought for a hundred bucks several years earlier. Everything would stain the microfiber, so cleaning it was a daylong event that would always result in aching shoulders, wrists, fingers and arms. So much so that I'd maybe only attempt it myself every few months and even then, preferably with a rented steam cleaner. My mother did it on her hands and knees. While I drank in the restorative mist of healing waterfall, my dying mother cleaned my couch.

When my mother died a few weeks after that weekend away, I blamed myself for not including her in the trip, for not being the type of person who would absolutely expend all the energy necessary to make sure their dying mother could have this one last comfort, to breathe in crisp mountain air and bathe in the ionic spray of a healing waterfall. If our positions were reversed, she would have found a way.

It was hard not to look at the couch and wonder if my own hypocrisy killed her. I said, come live with me and I will take care of you. Then I left her to scrub my house while I indulged in restoration, withholding it from her for the sake of my own serenity.

Agency

My grandmother died in the spring of 2018. Her death arrived two years after she buried her firstborn daughter, and seven months after I read *Migrants Against Slavery* at her bedside. She left to her inheritors a healthy middle class estate of several bank and investment accounts and her large suburban home. Altogether, the value of the inheritance was just under a million dollars.

This was her investment in her family, and her parting gift to all of us. Intangible to me because I hadn't relied on its comforts, it felt like play money. Imaginary. Everyone who lived in her house, it seemed, had already received their inheritance in some way or another anyway. Their housing, their water, their warmth, in some cases their vehicles and food, had all, for years, been subsidized by this not yet inherited inheritance.

Only my aunt and I had never taken up adult residencies in the house, and she alone paid for my grandmother's funeral.

Unfazed by the temporal promise of invisible, sure-to-be-contested cash from my grandmother's trust, I instead chose my own inheritance. At her wake, I took most of my grandmother's library of ancestry research home, including her copy of *Migrants Against Slavery*. It wasn't much; together, the few books and two large binders barely filled one third of a bookshelf. But the small stack was packed with personal ephemera. There were little notes folded into the pages of her books: barn and quilt codes used by the runaway enslaved, news articles from the 1850s, and transcribed in Grandma's inimitable script, names and numbers of recently discovered relatives. Her eight-year-old receipt from Powell's Books, yellowed but still legible.

Sorting through the documents, something hummed through my fingertips and up through my arms and chest before forming a lump in my throat. Were these notes for me?

After cycling through careers as a waitress, cook, secretary, and online marketer, I felt some pride in pivoting to my childhood ambition of writing. But at the time of my grandmother's death, my work consisted of bland copy written for bland businesses that surely no one would ever read unless necessary, and cannabis reviews that disappeared into the void of the internet with zero fanfare. Neither were jobs I could easily explain or justify to my grandmother. I wasn't entirely proud of the work I did; it felt like a selfish squandering of what might be a rare talent. Why would anyone who wasn't making money off of this type of disposable writing be proud of it either?

I fancied myself a compelling writer, but did my grandmother regard me in the same way? I never brought home a newspaper with my own byline, so I must wonder, did she regard me as a writer at all? Or was I as rudderless in her eyes as I was in my own?

Maybe before her death, my grandmother looked at my buttery complexion and knew my tenuous grasp on our heritage must be slipping as she shuffled into her next life. Maybe she was pushing these books into my hands for a reason deeper than research. Maybe she saw talents in me I had yet to see. Maybe she saw my mother in me in ways I'd yet to comprehend.

Perhaps somewhere in these pages she had hidden a key for me. A key that would make me better than the person who watched her mother die with a stone face. Better than the person who mooned an audience in fishnets and stilettos. Maybe there were instructions on how to carry on legacies, to share our vital stories, to live up to every expectation set forth by the previous generation.

Maybe my inheritance was here, maybe somewhere in these pages there was a guide to how to be a worthy ancestor.

****

On the eve of Ailsie's 12th birthday, the Fox Estate was visited by one of John's cousins, an English immigrant named Henry Newby. Henry was presumably traveling throughout the colonies, visiting family and friends, wondering where to sow his proverbial oats. His visit to the Fox estate was one stop on a several-year-long trip wherein Henry toured the amber waves of grain, the purple-mountain majesties, and the endless trade of human chattel between plantations.

While we know that Henry's visit to the Fox Estate coincided with Ailsie's approaching birthday, and that she would turn 12 years old over the course of his visit, the season is unrecorded. History recorded the whims of the Fox men, their romantic predilections, their fortunes, their waist sizes, but for Ailsie, an enslaved Black child, I only see vague whens and wheres as they relate to the men in her life. I never see whys or hows as they relate to her. I'm left to imagine everything about Ailsie. And it's a dearth of information that I fill with whimsical imaginings.

I wonder how Ailsie would have celebrated her birthday. If I belong to the fall, to crisp autumn days with warm breezes, the looming specter of Halloween influencing all my childhood birthday celebrations, what season did Ailsie belong to?

If Ailsie's birthday was in summer, would she have eaten cake outside? Would the farmhands and house servants all take a break to celebrate the budding adult within this child? How bright would the sun have shown on all of their faces, awash with sheens of perspiration? Were they sweating because of the weather or the work? Or both? What were their smiles like; wide and soft like my mother's? Did their demure grins drive deep dimples into their cheeks? And would their cheeks round out when their grins broke open, like my grandmother's would? When they broke out into song, whose voice was the loudest? And whose was the sweetest?

My mother's singing voice was rich and passionate. My grandmother's was airy and light. I sing out in a sturdy alto. Did they inherit those voices? Did I inherit mine?

If her birthday was encased in winter's stiff Atlantic winds and brief, ephemeral days, would Ailsie have huddled with other house servants in quiet celebration? Or would she have absconded to the quarters of the rest of her family to celebrate with unhushed liveliness? Did the cold affect her the same way it affects my sister, whose slight frame and chattering teeth are repelled by temperatures below 78 degrees, or did she revel in chilly temperatures the same way I do, forever turning her face toward the wind to feel its sharpness against her skin?

The precise dates of Henry's visit and of Ailsie's birthday and the seasons these events were defined by have been lost to time. What has been cemented into our family history, however, is that while touring the estate, Henry Newby saw a 12-year-old house servant named Ailsie and immediately turned to John Fox to ask if he could purchase her. His intent was to make her his wife.

The elementary school I attended in San Pedro was a small performing arts magnet dangling on the edge of the coastline. Once a month, classes would walk the three or four short blocks to the waterfront, where all the natural pools would reveal themselves when the tide was low, each pocket bustling with intertidal life. Starfish buckled and flexed in our hands, sea cucumbers squirted us with cool salt water, anemones gripped our fingertips as we dragged our little hands across their mouths, changing their shapes from splayed open flowers to swollen balls with pursed lips.

My sixth grade class took one such field trip. After examining the tide pools for a while, we sat on the rocky shore, in the shade of the sheer cliffs to our backs, and learned "My Bonnie." We sang it in rounds, giggling at the

nedians who were already

er ourselves to make our

this day, I lagged a few steps

ed in a particular tide pool,

many creatures as I could, obsessing

amas I imagined occurring in their tiny worlds.

man approached me from behind and tugged on my elbow in what would have been an obvious attempt at flirting if I'd had a more comprehensive frame of reference. I thought he was touching my arm because I was in trouble. He looked like he was older than a high-schooler, but younger than our teachers, the kind of in-between age of teenage movie stars. He asked my name and looked me up and down in a cocky way that felt like it was meant to congratulate me on holding his attention.

Was my distance from the group enough to erase my most childish characteristics? Or was this moment something nefarious and predatory?

A short distance down the beach, a teacher clapped and shouted for the kids' attention. She was attempting to recount the class before we headed into the series of chaparral switchbacks that would lead us back to the school. When she saw me, perhaps the tallest and most developed 12-year-old in her sixth grade class inching slowly backwards from a grown man who met each backward step with an approaching step of his own,

his lips curled with sensual inquisition, the sexu[al]
language of his body undeniable, she screamed.

He had only just asked my name, and as I rep[lied,]
her high shriek rang out from across the beach. In uniso[n]
I said "Brianna" just as my teacher screamed the same
name from a hundred yards away. In this moment, this
man heard the voice of a child, saw the horrified face of
her teacher, put his hands in the air in a signal of
surrender and dashed away, disappearing into memories,
not really even leaving his face behind.

Henry Newby saw a 12-year-old Ailsie and did not
see her as a child, or even simply a potential sexual
conquest. He saw her as a wife. A partner. Someone with
whom he might build a life.

I wonder if Ailsie, when removed from her peers,
really looked like a grown woman with some manner of
sexual agency. I was the most physically matured 12-year-
old in the neighborhood, constantly compelled to
practice a contrived maturity that met the expectation of
my size, but never my age. Did Ailsie feel the same? I was
so ashamed of my womanly body and the grotesque way
adults leered at me, their vulgar expressions tearing me
away from childhood by painting my every behavior with
a sexuality I was far too young to understand. Does that
shame run in the family? Would Ailsie and I commiserate
about it?

John Fox, father to many of his own slaves and certainly no stranger to the clandestine nature of slave/owner relations, told Henry that Ailsie was far too young to be sold off to someone who intended to have sexual relations with her. He told Henry to return to the estate in two year's time. If, after two years, he was still enamored by the child Ailsie, he could take her as a gift, but certainly not as a wife. Despite prolific evidence to the contrary, it was a high crime for a white person and a Black person to lay together.

To a 12-year-old, two years can feel eternal. For a 30-year-old, I imagine the time went by considerably faster. Henry returned two years to the date after his initial visit, and decided the time was well spent and that Ailsie was truly worth the wait. At the age of 14, she had grown into a stately young woman, a trait that, considering how I'd developed in the two years after the beach incident, ostensibly runs in the family.

And so John Fox gifted Ailsie to his cousin Henry, technically retaining his ownership to maintain the pretense that Ailsie was, in fact, still a slave, and not the child bride of a white land owner. Henry took his new paramour, bought 250 acres of undeveloped land in Culpeper County, and set out to start a new life with Ailsie. In another two years, their first son was born, a pale yellow baby born the color of a buttermilk biscuit.

They named him Dangerfield.

Home

A year after my grandmother's death, and a year before a drag queen's unboxing video inspired me to organize the chaos of her research, I returned to her home for the family's first holiday without her. I traveled with my husband and son from our home in Northeast Portland back to San Pedro. It's a daylong drive that we've taken many times. My mother would drive her 2001 White Ford Explorer back and forth no less than twice a year while she was alive. Sometimes with my grandmother, but often, she did it all alone.

There are two main ways to navigate from Portland to San Pedro. The easiest and most straightforward route is via Interstate 5, directly through the dry monotony of central California. The scenic route, on the other hand, traces the coastline, intermittently dipping into redwood forests and through quiet coastal towns, some with resort vibes, others too far removed from convenience to be considered luxury.

Before my grandmother's death, five people occupied her home with the intention of being her caregiver in some capacity. My cousin, her father, my sister, and my sister's family all took up space in Grandma's suburban three-bedroom house. From my considerable distance, it looked like each of these people were trying to stake some claim to my grandmother's estate, to establish a residency that couldn't be denied after her death, and maybe to inherit the house outright. Through my lens, altruism masked avarice, but I know there's no nuance in that perspective; I know it paints everything with a broad brush.

Approaching the home a year later, their presence was not a comfort. It was a reminder of all my grandmother left behind.

We stayed on Highway 101, the coast route, until LA traffic forced us onto Highway 110, a freeway that ends neatly about a mile from my grandma's house. We rode the freeway as it curved around the smoky dystopian skyline that is San Pedro, with its refineries to the east and massive port to the west.

As the utopian green foothills of Palos Verdes revealed themselves, purple clouds gathered and rain began pouring in sheets. My husband and I looked at each other from the corners of our eyes and sighed in unison, steeling ourselves for the onslaught of "Why'd you bring the rain with you?"

I could feel a soft panic percolating in my chest, and by the time we arrived at the Harbor Blvd off-ramp my palms were slick with sweat. I looked at our son in the backseat. Through the rear window, I could see a rainbow cascading from the parting rain clouds. It looked like it was landing right on his head. The "Welcome to San Pedro" pillar loomed behind him.

****

A few days earlier, as I packed for this trip, folding my son's tiny T-shirts, underwear, and shorts into neat stacks, I fantasized about filling a suitcase with only weed, forgoing clothes and toiletries for a bong and a mason jar of buds. Maybe a bikini and caftan. Grandma was the calm presence her home required, considering how loudly it bustled with entitled boarders. I anticipated that with those lodgers now fighting over sovereignty, even fabricated cool was better than the manic vibration I was maintaining in anticipation of being in their presence.

I'd been writing about weed for about a year, and had accumulated all manner of interesting products as a result. A younger me might have seen this work as ideal, but guilt gilded the edges of all my essays. I was refining my critical voice but it was happening at the expense of an entire generation of Black felons, convicted of doing arguably the same work that now legally paid my bills: pushing weed.

The more work I accepted, the more of an expert I became. If I had the clarity then, I would have reveled in becoming a new herald for ancestral plant medicine, a champion for nonviolent offenders of archaic cannabis laws, a voice for families shattered by the war on drugs. But my view was too narrow and my motivations too selfish to become anything more than a commentator, comparing gummies and filter-tip joints and craft cannabis/chocolate collaborations, encased in an artificial pride delivered care of the seemingly bottomless trove of samples I'd collected, which is to say, I was too stoned to be ashamed of how I was wasting my platform.

I thought of all the different types of cannabis I would need to maintain my glossy composure throughout a visit with this new incarnation of my same old family. Soon, my imaginary suitcase was stuffed with ridiculous items: a two-foot-tall bong, sticky ounces of top-shelf flower, an electric vaporizer for smoking several grams of wet gooey cannabis extract. I would need dozens of joints, because I'd be smoking at least a couple every morning, afternoon, and evening. I'd need boxes of medicated baked goods to maintain longer, more dissociative highs, and for variety's sake, I'd need a colorful assortment of soft and hard candies. I'd need a ceremonial pipe to smoke on the beach at sunset. Spoon pipes, lighters, papers, grinders. A bikini. A caftan.

My fantasy suitcase stayed packed in my mind. It was a cold comfort that cannabis was also legal in California. It's much more affordable in Oregon.

WHAT TO TAKE WHEN YOU DON'T WANT TO GO

1 a huge bong for daily "breathwork"

2 $500 e-rig for vaporizing concentrates

3 Assorted cookies I might get paid to review later

4 Oh my fuck, so many joints. Just, so many joints

5 Fire weed, juicy nugs, a hidden envelope of dabs

6 More lighters than I think I need. (And one in every pocket)

7 A spoon pipe just in case I need to smoke out a fool but
   I don't think they're worth a joint (sorry not sorry)

8 Novelty rolling papers for smoking other peoples weed

9 A shit ton of weed candy

10 Ceremonial Pipe

11 Caftans and panties ONLY .no pants.

It is the day before Christmas Eve when we arrive. With Grandma gone, this house has become lawless. I can tell as soon as we pull up to its pristine suburban curb that the place is in chaos. Each adjacent house is neater than the next, lawns manicured, gardens tended, sidewalks swept. If I hadn't grown up here, I might have noticed the suggestion of a creepy, Stepford-esque subdivision, but I'm too familiar, and my husband has to point it out to me. Not one blade of grass is out of place up and down the block.

But here, in front of my grandma's house, is an embarrassment of failed landscaping. My sister's husband has ripped the robust, vibrant flower garden my uncle planted for my grandmother from the front yard, and all this sudden heavy rain has made muddy puddles from the messy piles of soil.

As soon as we get out of our car, my sister rushes to meet us, looking balefully at the yard and muttering about a big landscaping project. I can tell from the way that she trails off that there are no plans. It was done in spite, a hostile act against our uncle's efforts.

She tells me she loathes our uncle. I feel like she's honed her animosity to a fine point during their cohabitation. To me, they've both done their part to destroy my fabricated ideal. Even in the wake of our grandmother's death, in my eyes, both my sister and uncle are unavailingly dependent on our deceased matriarch.

When my sister explains her experience in the house to me, I can't relate. My uncle will inevitably disappear, but her animosity will just transfer to the next person who stands between her and sole ownership of the house. This is what I see, but I don't think she would see it the same way. Even if we are each entitled to everything we want, our viewpoints are hundreds of miles apart.

I'm not sure how to nurture last generation's flowers, but I want to try. By contrast, she'd happily uproot them and leave them to rot.

I look at my grandmother's yard and realize I am also honing my opinions into points sharp enough to draw blood. The flowers were innocent victims of a family at odds over how to manage an inherited estate. Seeing them so unceremoniously ripped from the ground is a layer of grief my fragile psyche cannot support. Because of this, my weaponized opinions feel justified.

****

When I was 11, my family rented a home right up the street from my grandparents, three ranch-style houses away. My grandparents were the only Black homeowners on the block.

One year after we moved in, my father, in a softly secret way, came out of the closet by bringing his lover to my 13th birthday party and introducing him to our guests as his partner. Like most of the party, his coded, coming-out language was lost on me. My dad was entrepreneurial; we all just thought he had some new venture and this man was his new business partner. I was 13, so I spent most of the party in the bathroom dramatically crying over a crush anyway.

Shortly after the party, he and my mother arranged for a divorce, and he moved out of our home the following month. During the proceedings I would sneak into a hidden corner of the garage and cry silently in the dark so my mother wouldn't hear. I wanted to protect my mother and sister, who was five at the time. I wanted to rein in my father. In the years following the divorce my mother succumbed to the compounding tragedies of heartbreak, unchecked mental illness, and the scandalous circumstances of her single Black motherhood. For 12 hours a day she was a brilliant beacon, and at home she disappeared into shadows, barricading herself behind the door of her bedroom. But even before the divorce, I remember slivers of this behavior. I would see her shine brightly while she engaged other people's children, but wither and rage when she was home with me. Not all the time, but the polarity was too extreme to not stress me out. It was always there, but it reached a fever pitch after the divorce.

How could it not?

"That's just your mother," or some variation, my grandmother would say. And I would nod without ever understanding what that meant.

Meanwhile, in less than a year my father went from nebbish, closeted, middle-aged dad to rainbow flag-waving, pride parade-attending, established GAY®. The divorce granted my parents joint custody, and I spent most weekends with my father and his new partner, letting my dad's new life away from the suburbs inform a new life of my own. At home, my family was Black, suburban, and moderately evangelical; on the weekends, my community was full of refugees from suburban Christianity. This was a new chasm to straddle. On either side were neat lawns, Memorial Day BBQs, father figures, adopted mothers, play cousins. On both sides there were values that prioritized love and acceptance, on both sides there was shame, but the conditions were so different.

I sat in the murky middle of those cultures, unsure of how my identities intertwined, or how to navigate the deep divides between them.

Performing normalcy atop fractured foundations was something the members of my father's new community had in common. I learned that there existed a language for children forced into maturity by less than gracious shepherds. I was trapped between who I thought I was supposed to be and who I actually was, searching for a place to fit in, and exhausted from trying. This community was exceedingly relatable.

I left my mother's home for the last time when I was 16. It wasn't a big dramatic eruption, and I didn't escape in some blaze of glory. One day I just left for my father's house and didn't come back. Then I left for my mother's house and didn't come back. It was months before either knew I had left the other's care. I slept on friends' couches or crashed with lovers too old to be messing with someone my age. No one noticed. My mother was lost in a ping pong between performance and exhaustion, and my father was lost in his liberation. Neither existence left a tremendous amount of room for me, a smart, calm, independent child who, in another time, might have already been a wife and mother herself.

So my new life began without celebratory graduations or rites of passage. At 16, I took a proficiency test that allowed me to move on from high school to an Associate's Degree program at the local community college, effectively "graduating" one year early. Or dropping out, depending on your point of view. I crashed on couches, partying away weeks at a time. I paid for a few college classes out of my pocket, and my grandmother paid for a few as well, but I also paid for a lot of hard drugs and liquor. I quickly bailed on my college classes, too strung out to participate. Again, neither parent noticed.

My mother and my sister moved to a new house a few years later, and my mother began the exacting process of re-writing her own motherhood by parenting my sister, nearly a decade my junior, with all the tenderness, understanding, and attention she withheld from me. From the outside, it looked like it wasn't enough for my father to be cleaved from her life for her to heal; I had to be carved out as well.

After I cleaned myself up and re-enrolled in college, I told her during an argument that she treated motherhood like baking a cake. That she seemed disappointed with her first try, so she diverted all her attention to the second go. For a moment she looked affronted, but then her face dissolved into something I was very familiar with: pride. She was impressed by how apt my metaphor was.

My resentment has evolved and redirected itself. In my youth, the abandonment was her fault, her moods were wild and unpredictable, how was I supposed to handle her? Now, I see the fault as mine. I felt rejected by her when I embraced my father's new life, so I just rejected her back. A petty addition to what was already more than she could manage. The truth was, I hadn't rejected her then, when I disappeared myself from her care, but when I looked into the face of a Black Barbie and grimaced.

Were the behaviors that divided us reactions to that rejection? How much damage had I done by rejecting her painfully hypocritical Christian evangelical values? How much more damage did I do by rejecting her pain?

First, I had chosen not to be Black, then I rejected heteronormativity, then I rejected her. Now I must untangle myself from those decisions and the ripples they left behind. This too is an inheritance.

In all the years since I left, I've had the persistent nightmare that I'm running down the clean concrete squares of the San Pedro sidewalk between my grandmother's house and the house that I grew up in, hiding in hedges from my family, fearing some mysterious retribution, and feeling like no one in the world can help me. I often wake up from this dream in tears.

Now, every time I walk along the sidewalk between the houses, I feel like my entire body is puckering, like I'm being squeezed from the inside. All I can do is shut my eyes and wait for the feeling to pass.

****

Being flooded with neighborhood memories is overwhelming, and the inside of my deceased grandmother's house is just as unsettling. A piece of my grandmother's wall art has been replaced with a wood-burned portrait of my sister in a windswept occult-themed landscape, perhaps not overtly wicked, but certainly on the shadowy side of esoteric. Charred details of pentagrams and animal skulls stand out, and I wonder how my cousin, whose grip on the house's Christian status quo is fierce, feels about this genre of fine art.

The gallery wall that greeted everyone who entered the home has always been dedicated to family pictures. Grainy and old, new and glossy, laser printed, all of them neatly framed regardless. Now, a single painted portrait of my sister's family stands out; it's replacing someone's picture but I can't recall whose. The paintings and woodburnings are delicate, lovely pieces of art, and would be charming enough in a home my sister and husband established themselves, but on our evangelical grandmother's walls they seem more than out of place; they seem disrespectful. To me these portraits seem to say, "finally, this house is mine."

Select pictures of me in childhood are gone. The parlor piano that for decades was a focal point of the living room is gone. To me at least, that piano was integral to this home. It was where my grandmother first taught me the scales. A pile of shoes and empty storage boxes occupy the space where it had most recently sat.

The decrepit collection of Louis L'Amour paperbacks from my childhood are still neatly stacked on the bookshelf at the top of the staircase. Grandma loved the Wild West.

My sister and her husband have assumed my grandparent's bedroom, and as I peer inside to see how much the room has changed, I'm struck with a memory of my sister, my mother, and me watching TV in this room a few years prior.

My mother was sitting in a camping chair in the corner, crocheting or maybe knitting, while my sister and I were sprawled on the bed. The room was crowded with Grandma's ephemera: jewelry boxes atop dressers, overflowing with gold chains and costume gems. Wigs pinned to styrofoam heads lined the bookcase headboard of her ornate bed frame, which once housed a waterbed, but now held a standard mattress. Opulent furs, colorblocked suits and church hats poked out from behind a wall of sliding, mirrored closet doors that could never quite shut over their contents.

I was seven months pregnant and stretching my legs over my head, absentmindedly loosening my hips so that I might someday be able to do a spontaneous split. My sister, who'd just given birth to her first son not quite a year earlier, looked at me agape and said, "Wow, even before I had Dex I couldn't stretch like that," and without looking up our mother said, "it's because she does yoga," elongating and intoning the word *yoga* with a songbird-sweet melody.

YOoooOOoooOOgaaaAAHhhhh

It's one of my favorite memories of the three of us, but this is no longer that room. That room no longer exists.

****

Five years before my family arrived for our first post- grandma Christmas visit, over cocktails with my aunt, cousin, and sister in a Las Vegas hotel room, our conversation turned to Grandma's age and her health. She had recently overcome breast cancer but was also experiencing a kind of waterfalling of ailments that she explained away as part and parcel of living past 85. At that time, my mother, cousin, and uncle were all living in her house, presumably with the intention of being of service to her.

We postulated Grandma's death in a way that felt plain and rational.

My cousin asked if I would ever move back to San Pedro, if I would ever want to take over ownership of Grandma's house to raise a family of my own.

I considered the question. If I had no cousin or sister or aunt or uncle, no one else to share the inheritance with, then sure, I'd spend a year or two in San

Pedro restoring the house before selling it. Maybe I'd finally learn to surf or kayak. The house was certainly close enough to the ocean. Hypothetically, the transition wouldn't be difficult for my young son, my husband would probably find work easily, and maybe, on some subconscious level, I wouldn't feel ghosts judging my pale existence from the corners of every room.

In a moment of vulnerability, I gave in to the pure fantasy that I was the lone inheritor of my grandmother's gifts, but before I could articulate my weirdly reasoned, weed- and champagne-charged "yes," my sister theatrically cut me off. She began waving her arms like a referee, heaving in and out of her overstuffed hotel chair as if she was too upset for her body to contain her emotions.

"No! No! I call bullshit! I call bullshit on you right now! You said you would never move back! You literally said *never*. No fucking way. Total bullshit." She was getting aggressive. The mood of the room turned sour.

"Oh, so the only valid fantasy is the fantasy where you inherit the house then?" I said, my face hardening. I wasn't expecting the conversation to twist into this weird confrontation.

"You wouldn't and you won't! You don't even want to live there." She was maintaining a hyper-performative, melodramatic pitch I found repellant. She kept it up as I

76

walked away, back to the adjoining hotel room she and I shared.

That night, I laid awake, simmering in bitter acrimony.

The house should be sold as soon as Grandma passes, I thought. If my sister's unhinged reaction was any indication, anything less would result in an embarrassingly revolting battle between entitled adults.

My grandparents' middle-class estate was generational wealth with intangible potential. Their single-family Los Angeles home was worth five houses in places less proximate to the Hollywood sign and the Redondo Beach Pier. This inheritance was meant to be shared. It was an unequivocal fantasy that any one of us would simply inherit this house outright, a fantasy to indulge over cocktails. Their estate was meant to be our new business ventures, our cross-country relocations, our children's college funds. But it seemed like all everyone else saw was one suburban house. And even now, in hypotheticals during cocktail hour, some were willing to brawl for it.

In that moment, I felt like a funhouse mirror reflection of the self I'd cultivated away from these imaginary discussions of wealth and propriety. And the reflection was complex to the point of dread. One self sees roses to be cultivated tenderly, but the reflection sees invasive roots that must be pruned. Another self sees opportunity in the petals, but her reflection sees it in the loose earth.

We all know our legacies are but one golden thread in the tapestry we weave of our existence. We all know blossoms die, and some roots run shallower than others, but I think that what we weave and what we cultivate is up to us, alone.

Maybe I'm wrong.

****

I turn my back on what is now my sister's bedroom, and my fingers twitch with unfulfilled anticipation. I walk back down the stairs and to the right, looking for my grandmother's piano, my one constant comfort in the house.

I find it in the garage. The piano has been relinquished not just to this dark dusty room, but to the bottom of a very tall pile of storage boxes, its keys completely inaccessible.

Every year I'd learn a new holiday carol by ear, and one of my purest joys was playing them for Grandma, on Grandma's piano, in Grandma's house. I'd been playing piano with Grandma since childhood, but in an effort to learn to read and write music, I'd started taking piano classes after her death. I'd learned to play "Auld Lang Syne" and was hoping to play it for our family on New

Year's Eve, the night before we would return home to Portland.

The prospect of this year's failed tribute makes my heart skip a beat, but more than that, it feels like a crucial part of myself, who has as much of a claim to this home as any of the residents, has also been relegated to storage.

I should say something. I should kick open the garage door, march right up to my sister and cousin and tell them they are fucking up our legacy, burying treasures under garbage, spitefully ripping out our roses, playing nice as if they aren't stuck in an everlasting loop, forever sharing a house too small for them all but too large for only one, forever pecking at each other to establish order, neither one the matriarch they seem to want to be. I should remind them of all the dreams our grandmother had for us. I should remind them of the dreams they had for themselves.

I should show them what I see: potential for all of us to live a life of our own making. What our grandmother wanted. They are two traumatized women locked in the same cycle of dependency as their parents. I see it all coming, and I can stop it right now.

But I don't. I choose not to.

Instead, I fold into myself, aching to melt into the ground beneath me. I feel like all of my ancestors are looking down on me saying, "You? All of our suffering, our mettle, our losses, it comes down to you? And these are the choices you make? You sit here mute when words could be the salve that saves your family? Talk to them, cry to them, shout, stomp your feet, demand they hold you up while you grieve out loud.

"Why do you use your privilege to hide?"

I hunch at the piano, piled high with cardboard boxes, dusty and inaccessible. I feel like a sieve, all my potential slowly draining from me, wasted. I'm not the stage performer my grandmother defended to San Pedro High School's drama department, I'm not a reflection of my mother's altruism and brilliance. I'm not the strong sister my family needs as it navigates this new grief. I'm not the daughter that brought us closer together. I'm not the calm reflective lake.

I don't know what or who or why I am.

What contributions have I made, to this family, to the world? I can't think of any. I haven't lived up to any of my mother's or my grandmother's expectations, and now that they are both dead I'll never get the chance. This piano will turn to dust in this garage. I was its steward and it's going to turn to dust. I begin to spiral.

I can't pull myself out of this trench. I'm sinking deeper.

Walking through that overcrowded house, seeing my treasured piano buried under a dozen half-empty storage boxes, tripping over gaping holes where flowers once thrived, and wondering why my family would rather fight for scraps than invest in new beginnings. But I won't ask them. So I can't help but feel like, maybe, none of us are worth it.

The REDACTED Estate includes:

- House at ### Englander St. San Pedro, CA and all its contents
- X Savings and Y Investment Accounts

And is to be divided as follows:

The Children's Trust:
REDACTED (RIP) 16% of all assets (to be passed to daughters)
REDACTED 16% of all assets
REDACTED 16% of all assets

The Grandchildren's Trust:
REDACTED 16% of all assets
Brianna 24% of all assets (including mother's share)
REDACTED 24% of all assets (including mother's share)

On Christmas Eve, I wake up morose. All throughout my grandmother's house, I am compelled to ask myself why I am crawling out of my skin. This place should be a sanctuary to me, but everything just feels repellent. It is more than the portraits on the walls, the missing piano, the swamp in the front yard; it is something deeper, something in the infrastructure that is rotted.

I smoke a joint and meditate on these feelings. I want to investigate them, and maybe soothe them, so that I can articulate them. I want them to make sense. The rabbit hole begins at resentment, then spins off into shame. I suppose I feel shame over my ability to move through the world with a privilege never afforded to our grandparents. And I am ashamed I've done so little with it. I am resentful of the unearned entitlement that hung over us, and regretful I haven't learned to exploit it.

Perhaps that is the rot that makes this ground feel weak beneath my feet.

I sit down with my cousin to have a cup of tea, tighten up our holiday plans, and catch up as cousins do. She tells me anecdotes about her ex-husband and muses about re-landscaping the messy front gardens.

At this point, she has already been living in my grandmother's house for several years. I can see by her body language that, since my grandmother's passing, she seems possessed by some matriarchal energy that, awkwardly, does not suit her.

I don't want to wear it either.

My estranged uncle's only child, my cousin is older than me by seven years. She lived most of her childhood with my grandparents. Given our proximity, our relationship has the tenor of big sister/little sister but the rhythm of city cousin/country cousin, her views sometimes coming off as shortsighted and ignorant, and conflicting with mine, shaped by my father's advocacy and my mother's commitment to her culture.

Every time we visit, we sit for long, personal chats. We fill each other in on the drama and the joys of everyday lives. But I'm far more withholding than I would lead her to believe. Because of this, she sees me as stoic and strong. I express very little in terms of my own emotions, but readily make myself available as a sounding board for her, an empty well eager to absorb someone else's troubles rather than admit my own.

Our chat begins genially; we catch up on the goings on of our extended family. Who's getting married? Who's pregnant? My cousin mentions guests she'll host while my family is staying there, and I cringe. The house is crowded enough without the residents acting on their accommodation fantasies. My sister has also invited a friend to stay. I see both of their invitations as laying a claim, as if to say "This is my house now, I am in charge, so of course whoever I like can stay for as long as they like." Neither of them seem to have considered that I might not feel as comfortable with this arrangement as they are.

The conversation then takes a strange turn. Despite the fact that my cousin lives in a house she's inherited, she asks me, "Since when do homeless people have rights?" before launching into a jokey tirade about how a friend of hers had to shoo a houseless couple from her back alley garage entrance. Only here do I interject, to tell her that all of us are only one, maybe two tragedies away from being houseless ourselves, and if it bothers her so deeply, I can help her find ways to contribute to a solution. I still have many advocacy-minded friends in the area.

Changing the subject, she moves on to asking me what will happen with my child when I'm too old to care for him. I correct her and tell her autism is not monolithic, development isn't linear, we won't know what our son is capable of until he gets "there," but that doesn't mean that he won't get "there."

Explaining autism is tiring, and I feel the conversation sliding into a territory that turns my stomach. Though my mother loved them, teachable moments exhaust me, and I am still reeling from my cousin's homeless comment.

I ask her how living with my sister has been, and she begins to unpack the processes of caring for my grandmother in the months, weeks, and days before her death. She praises my sister and recounts how well they worked together as caregivers. It's heartwarming on its surface. I know they did everything they could to make our grandmother's passing as painless as possible. She tells me in trembling tones how difficult Grandma's care was and how proud and impressed she was by my sister's empathy and nerve. They were a perfect team then, accepting, even enthusiastic, about their fates as cohabitants. Even in their distaste for my uncle, my cousin's father, who my cousin says contributed very little in terms of my grandmother's care, they were simpatico.

I make a forgettable comment, "Huh, fathers..." It's not a remark with a beginning or an end, it's just an echo.

"You said it, Cousin, *fathers*." She says *fathers* while pulling a sneer. It's meant for comic effect but it lands a bit too true to be worth a chuckle. She begins to tell me about something that happened the year my dad came out of the closet, when she returned to my grandparent's house after an extended stay in Texas. She arrived to find my grandmother quietly weeping over the washing machine in the garage. She asked my grandmother what was wrong, and my grandmother said, "The worst thing. The worst thing that could ever happen to a woman happened to your aunt." And my cousin says she knew at that instant, and said out loud to our grandmother, "Oh my god, Brianna's dad is gay."

I've never heard this story. Listening to it now is shattering my heart. I've only been back in my grandmother's house, back on the block I grew up on, for a couple of hours when my cousin recalls this memory for me with the gossipy-casualness of a nosy neighbor. She reminisces over the conversation as if I have grown beyond an emotional response to such a recollection.

Sometimes I tell the story of my father's coming out, and I think people laugh and cringe because, when told with emotional detachment, it's a funny anecdote. Maybe though, they cringe because, when considered from the vantage point of a 12-year-old child already tenuously straddling the fence between contentious cultures, the punchline, "And so, for my birthday, instead of half Black and half white, I graduated to half Black and half gay," is a bit more harsh than it is playful.

That self-deprecation is self defense. And every corner I turn in this house makes me think it's a defense against something here, some indefinable energy that hums heavily in this atmosphere. I feel entitled to this space, but I also feel like I don't belong here. Something foundational to who I am was structurally damaged here, and what was built on top feels ramshackle; a crumbling wooden roller coaster on an overactive faultline. Grandma's death was the event that finally sent the whole affair crashing into the earth.

My cousin keeps talking, and my foundation keeps crumbling. I don't want to be here anymore.

When my mother and father split up, my mother spent years detached emotionally from her children; she would spew venom at the mention of my father, and I took every comment personally. She'd wail about how alone she was, and I would wonder why she would say those things when I was standing right there, desperate to comfort her. She was a middle-aged Black woman drowning in the quicksand of depression and misdiagnosed mental illness and generational trauma. But, it was somehow the uniquely taboo trauma of being walked out on by a gay husband that became her most defining wound.

As my cousin looks at me, content in her chatting, I scream internally. How was a lover coming out of the closet the worst thing that can happen to a woman? If her children were alive and healthy, if she had all the unconditional support of her community, if her former lover was dutifully dedicated to his responsibilities as a father, how is a mostly amicable divorce the worst thing that could happen?

My cousin moves onto another topic, but it doesn't matter; I've tuned her out and fixed my expressions to autopilot. I am 13 years old again and I know, without a doubt, that I do not matter. I know that if my dad had stayed in the closet, and instead I died a terrible death, well, apparently, it wouldn't be the worst thing.

I don't know if these inner screams are directed at my cousin's nonchalance or the memory of my mother, who, in the backswamps of her mental illness, had kind of abandoned me too.

These are the unreasonable thoughts of a 13-year-old, but they're still dictating how I feel about this house, this family. Why was the worst thing they could imagine homosexuality? How could a family that survived the atrocities I read about in my grandmother's devastating genealogy research consider this the worst thing that could happen to a woman?

I have queer inclinations I kept secret my entire life because I thought I had evidence that my family may come to resent me, maybe even hate me for them. Now my cousin has spoken those evidences into truth.

I thought about my son's recent diagnosis, and in light of my grandmother's reaction to my father's coming out, my teenage heart twisted a prediction about what her reaction to my son's diagnosis might be. Would it be God's fault? Would it be mine? Would it be the worst thing that can ever happen to a mother?

A few weeks after he was born, when I was finally ready to receive guests, she and my mother drove up together to meet him. My grandmother held him for the first time, and looked into his eyes. He stared back. Without looking up, apropos of nothing, my grandmother said, "You're his everything."

On its face, it was a cute aphorism; I didn't take it as advice. But now I see that it was. But even though it seems like everything she did was done for her children, she was still a mother whose own intolerances bled into her relationships in ways she'd never been aware of. If I am my son's everything, when do my own intolerances bleed into his? When will they become his worst thing?

The subject of my cousin's father comes up when, desperate for something low stakes she can grab on to, I ask about his newest paramour, a woman we met briefly at my grandmother's service. We share a chuckle over how instead of introducing her to his family during our grandmother's wake, he stole her away to his sparse upstairs bedroom where they awkwardly ate from paper plates they balanced on their knees. I admire my cousin's mettle when she speaks about her father. I have no relationship with him but, to me, the atmosphere suggests he took advantage of our grandmother. From my viewpoint, it seems that my sister and cousin celebrate his absence as if that were true.

However, from my vantage point, not one person who lives in this house is innocent of that charge. Everyone has taken advantage of my grandmother. My lens is wide angle. Too much truth is cropped out of everyone else's closeup frame.

The last time I saw my uncle was when I had flown down to help with the setup for Grandma's at-home palliative care. He had left a note on my cousin's bed, not knowing I was staying in her room, that said, "I got stage 4 stomach cancer. Keep my name out your mouth and stay out of my business."

I gave the note to my cousin, and she threw it in a wastebasket where it sat, plainly open, for the rest of my stay.

Now, I give her an audience, and she relays her frustrations over her own father. I sip tea, and breathe deeply to steady my thrashing heart.

****

Christmas morning, I spend time playing with my son and nephew on a newly planted strip of grass in the mostly paved backyard. My nephew is barely a year older than my son, and he has lived in my grandmother's house for most of his life.

My sister maintained that her residency in San Pedro was impermanent when she moved her family into the master bedroom, displacing my grandmother to the den. She would rehash the same five-year plan to me again and again – that she and her husband and son would be moving to North Hollywood, or maybe even Paris, where she would pursue her education and a career in couture.

My grandmother never complained. She seemed genuinely happy to have them there.

When my sister describes her goals, she speaks with an entitlement that I can't relate to because she's been taken care of in a way that I haven't. Her wants are justified because they are her wants, and they should be met because they've always been met. A large house, a luxury car, a six-figure education - these are all logical desires for her, but seem like astronomical aspirations to me. I can't even hypothesize how many hours over how many years I would have to work in order to afford any of the things she takes for granted. When I focus in on the fractures that divide us, I think I see my parents' course correction with her, having ostracized me with tandem bouts of terrifying suicidal depression and newly-out, living-my-gay-truth self absorption. But it feels like they overshot the mark; I see my sister as coddled, and myself as hardened and avoidant, as a result.

My sister's aspirations are in conflict with how she's chosen to live. She's well taken care of, yet she rails against anyone she assumes is wealthy. Her rages feel to me like a mimicry of the anti-gay rhetoric my mother would spew over my father in my presence; a principled blindness that obscures what does not suit the narrative. Our mother was an artist and activist, she had many gay friends, but in the context of her own personal life, homosexuality was a tragedy. To critique wealth in an inherited home is as asinine as critiquing the poverty of people you've never met is as absurd as railing against homosexuality to your gay BFF. The views held by the residents of this home are narrow enough to exclude everyone but their own reflections, and the house is falling apart as a result.

I look at my nephew and wonder how the energy of this house affects him. I see myself in him. He looks at me with a face so obviously related to mine, and an exhaustion I think I recognize. When I made that face, it was because I wanted to protect my mother, but I didn't understand what she needed protecting from.

On the night of our first Christmas dinner without Grandma, we welcome our extended family to the house for a large sit-down meal. There is a turkey, extra buttery mashed potatoes, glossy brown gravy, a pot of collard greens, a tray of macaroni and cheese complete with crispy edges, biscuits, pies, salads and ham. I am in charge of the turkey, and though each dish has been delegated, my husband and I take on the lion's share of the work. It's a small kitchen.

Being trusted with the majority of the cooking is an honor. I spent the morning fretting over the meal, the timing, the guests, and a 30-pound turkey my cousin bought that barely fit in the oven, but spacing out in the kitchen for several hours was peaceful. The one window in the kitchen was above the sink, looking out onto the backyard. I remembered catching my grandmother gazing at me as a child while she did the dishes and I played outside. I was swinging her rake around and pretending I was Cheetara from the *ThunderCats*. Now it was me gazing at my son as he and his cousin laid in that same yard to watch clouds crawl across the bright blue sky.

My son is comfortable in my grandmother's house. He knows his way around the rooms, how to get in and out of the backyard. He knows how to operate the remote controls for each of the televisions in each of the rooms. He knows how to navigate to his favorite shows so he can watch the introductory credits over and over and over on a loop.

I explained to my nephew, "Rainier doesn't watch TV or play games the way we do – you just hafta kinda go with it." He nodded and we shrugged together in shared nonchalance.

Just as this house was assumed a sanctuary for me, I wanted that extended to my own son. Everyone else in this family seemed to feel ownership of these spaces, these walls. Why shouldn't he?

But the houseguests my cousin and sister had invited to stay for the holidays cut their eyes at the chaotic way my son existed in the house's shared spaces. One, a grade-school teacher, asked me how I felt about the stigma they assumed my son and I would carry our entire lives, then told me how special education is a lane few grade school teachers even want to look down. Another, a white 19-year-old girl, asked for a poverty tour of Los Angeles' skid row one night, citing a love for urban decay. I held my breath and imagined what my grandmother's or my mother's reactions would be to either of those statements. They were so graceful during teachable moments, but in that moment I just felt rage. I felt rage because, in a house I was already uncomfortable in, the residents wouldn't stop making me more uncomfortable. Rather than engage any of them, I withdrew.

I wanted to think that my grandmother wouldn't have allowed either guest to stay while I was there with my own family.

So, I eat 50 mg of cannabis before I start cooking, and the high keeps redirecting my thoughts to the window, to watch my son play with his cousin. I wonder what their conversations will be like when they are grown enough to have something to look back on.

The dinner is as much a success as it is a failure. My sister's guest usurps my seat, the last open chair at the head of the table, just as I lay down the last dish. Not my cousin or my sister or any other family member says anything. Everyone just begins eating as I stand off to the side, watching, incredulous. I fix a plate and walk through the banquet tables we set up in the living room, past the kids table, past the pile of shoes where the piano used to be, and into the den. My husband leaves the table as soon as he realizes I hadn't freely offered my seat to my sister's guest.

I could say something, but instead I just try to disappear.

Really, I want more than to just disappear. I want to cease to exist. I'd spent so many holiday dinners in that same room, alone, crying over something someone had said about my homo dad, or my crazy mom, or how overdeveloped I was, or how weird I was. My head swells with memories of rejection and frustration and embarrassment.

I've agreed to keep my family there until New Year's because I'd committed to helping throw a NYE family fête. I shudder with regret. I would leave in the morning if I thought I could. I seethe at the sound of my family laughing in the dining room without me. There are still five more days left in this trip.

Dangerfield

I've heard his name over and over for most of my life. He was a hero to my grandma, and an idol to our family. In her eyes, she thought we should all aspire to be as brave, as brilliant, as resilient, and as devoted as the immortal Dangerfield, the first of John Brown's raiders to die during the raid on Harpers Ferry.

Growing up, none of my Black friends knew Dangerfield. His name never came up in any of my American History classes. Even in my community college African-American history class, his name was never mentioned.

If – and that's a big if – you learned about the raid on Harpers Ferry in school, or in an African-American history community college class worth three credits, John Brown was undoubtedly the main element of the lesson.

John Brown as in:

Glory, Glory, Hallelujah
Glory, Glory, Hallelujah

Glory, Glory, Hallelujah
His soul goes marching on

That John Brown. The one whose body lies a-mouldering in his grave.

The raid on Harpers Ferry, as my grandmother told it, was the battle that started the American Civil War– the war that ended slavery – and Dangerfield was the shining hero. This event took place in 1859, at the United States Federal Armory in Harpers Ferry, Virgina, and occurred between a motley army of abolitionists and a chaotic assemblage of pro-slavery militias and U.S. military forces over the course of two days. The raiders had overtaken the armory with plans to abscond with weapons, arm the enslaved, and light the fuse of an American insurrection. The raiders, including Dangerfield, were led by Brown.

John Brown was the infamous white abolitionist who, during his time, some thought to be a second coming of Moses. He's often mentioned in the same breath as famed abolitionist Frederick Douglass or Baptist-minister-cum-freedom-fighter Nat Turner. His infamy percolated in the territory that would become Kansas.

The status of Kansas was critical. Whether it became a pro-slavery state or a free state would shift the balance of a Senate split between free states and states committed to sustaining the enslavement of humans. The stakes were higher than Kansas; the stakes were humanity. And between 1854 and 1859, Brown and other free-state settlers fought pro-slavery militias in and around the proposed state over the legality of slavery. The battles were brutal, and entire towns were destroyed as a consequence. Houses burnt down, communities leveled.

Settlers in Kansas, where Black folks were offered land grants, overwhelmingly hoped to establish a free state, but slavery-sympathetic senators fought for Kansas to enter the union as a slave state. Bands of pro-slavery attackers, mostly Missourian "border ruffians," were encouraged to violently menace the settlers. Two raids leveled the town of Lawrence, which was founded as a headquarters of the free state ideal. During the first raid in 1856, two buildings were burnt down and one person died. In the second raid, seven years later, more than 150 people were killed and Confederates burned at least a quarter of the town.

In retaliation, John Brown, who had relocated from New York to Kansas with five of his twenty children to fight pro-slavery forces, raised an anti-slavery company large enough to cut through the pro-slavery settlements of Pottawatomie Creek in Kansas, murdering five settlers by slicing their bodies to pieces with long swords. Militias intent on a pro-slave western expansion replied by shooting Brown's son, Fredrick, in broad daylight, and burning down the Brown family house.

The pro-slavers then raided the settlement of Osawatomie, and John Brown, gathering men along the way, met them there to fight. He and his men were overcome, and Osawatomie was burned to the ground. This was the roiling precursor to the Civil War, a pre-war period dubbed Bleeding Kansas, where John Brown's legacy crystalized. He became notorious enough to be nicknamed "The Old Terrifyer."

Despite the loss of the settlement, John Brown's defense of Osawatomie against tremendous odds earned him another more personal, proudly held nickname: Osawatomie Brown.

John Brown's mythology paints the picture of an austere, strapping white man with very thin lips and a stiff, brickish head. In images, he appears both a bit frightening and a bit biblical. He has a preacher's posture, wooden but consolatory, and a hard, penetrating gaze that burns through every portrait I've ever seen of him.

John was a deeply religious man. He famously swore, "I have only a short time to live, and only one death to die. I will die fighting for this cause. There will be no peace in this land until slavery is done for." It's probably his most popular pull quote – it appears in every article or book I've ever read about him.

In 1861, Kansas gained its inclusion to the union as a free state. Two years earlier, in 1859, Brown rented a property in Maryland, about five miles away from the Virginia town of Harpers Ferry, where a prodigious US government weapons factory stood ready for his capture. Or liberation.

The property Brown rented was called the Kennedy Farm. It's worth noting that after John Brown and his company's occupation made it famous, the Kennedy Farm would become a Black Elks lodge, and later, a hot ticket on the chitlin' circuit, which, for the uninitiated, is a nationwide tour's worth of Black-owned, -operated, and -patronized nightlife venues east of the Rocky Mountains. At the time, however, Kennedy Farm was a log cabin described as "Rough, unsightly." It was a very plain farmhouse cabin, with two main spaces: the lower containing a kitchen, parlor and dining room, and the upper holding sleep chambers, storage, a drilling room, and a prison.

In the weeks following Brown's settlement, his followers quietly traveled from Kansas to meet him. For more than a year Brown had traversed the northern states on his way to Maryland, collecting firearms and followers, developing his plan to overtake the armory at Harpers Ferry: he would lead a company of men into the town, snatch a number of influential townspeople from their homes in the dead of night, relay their plan to their prisoners' slaves, and then return their prisoners to the armory.

Brown was armed with 950 specially-made pike-heads. They looked like the steel blades of a spear tip, and were meant to be weapons for the raiders and the newly freed.

In 1859, weeks before his raid on Harpers Ferry, John Brown took a meeting with Frederick Douglass. They argued for two days. Douglass insisted that this plan was destined to fail, pushing the cause of abolition backward, tightening shackles, and reenforcing slavery's stronghold on the nation.

Brown was resolute that he and his company would abscond from the armory with as many firearms as they could muster and arm as many slaves as they could as they raided plantations to the south, leading to an uprising that would end in total abolition. John Brown expected many slaves would enthusiastically join, and that his army would soon become an unstoppable force: an instrument of God.

Two other men attended that meeting between Brown and Douglass: John Henry Kagi, John Brown's secretary, and a compatriot of Douglass, a fugitive from slavery named Shields Green. Brown was enthusiastic about his odds, and orated with passion as he implored Douglass to join. Green looked on.

In his autobiography, Douglass recalls how this meeting with Brown convinced Green to join the company. He recalled that Brown promised to defend him with his own life, and that Douglass could be the mouthpiece to the effort that ended slavery. "But my discretion or my cowardice made me proof against the dear old man's eloquence-perhaps it was something of both which determined my course. When about to leave I asked Green what he had decided to do, and was surprised by his coolly saying, in his broken way, 'I b'leve I'll go wid de ole man.'"

Dangerfield Newby came into Brown's company earlier that year; they were both lodged with Underground Railroad custodian, T. Smith Edwards. Dangerfield lived in Bridgeport, Ohio, a critical point in the network. The same altruistic blood that ran through my mother and grandmother's hearts ran in his as well; he's said to have been dedicated to the railroad's support. It was while he was building up his bankroll to buy the freedom of his wife, working as a blacksmith for Edwards' brother, that he met John Brown.

A shared associate named Alfred Hawkes introduced Dangerfield to John while they were all at the home of Edwards. John reportedly replied, "We aren't buying men."

Visualizing that moment, I'm indignant for Dangerfield. How dare John Brown assume this saint of a man, the man sanctified by my grandmother, presented himself to be bought or sold? How dare he think Dangerfield matched his gaze with anything other than commensurate passion?

Though, I only speculate John's inference. Perhaps the statement was not an assumption, but a warning that joining John Brown only paid dividends in blood.

In my mind's eye, I imagine the two of them meeting, shaking hands and looking deep into each other's eyes, communicating pleasantries on the surface that belied an intense subconscious connection formed from beliefs they shared, simultaneously seeing something in each other that lit fires within them.

Later, maybe over a shared dinner, I bet Dangerfield heard the same impassioned speech Brown gave Frederick Douglass and Shields Green. I imagine that speech was rehearsed, like a pastor rehearses a sermon. Or, like an instrument of God, maybe it erupted from him like lava from a volcano, every time the same but every time different.

And Brown would know he was preaching to his choir. Dangerfield was the first-born son of a white land owner and his enslaved child bride, whose limited autonomy was dictated by where and to whom his body was leased. He was a man with a wife and children who were owned by a different man who, when confronted with the prospect of that wife and those children's freedoms, deemed no price too high. Dangerfield was a man with an enormous extended family, raised in an evangelical community, with so many members owned and leased and bought and sold by wicked men.

Dangerfield was a man who might believe in an instrument of God made mortal, and he was probably convinced to follow John Brown into a righteous battle long before they'd even met.

Brown's raiding party, once assembled, contained about 22 members in total: a small group of Kansas abolitionists that had followed Brown after the Pottawatomie Creek massacre, three of Brown's surviving sons, and five free Black men, three of whom were mixed: John Copeland, Lewis Leary, Osborne Perry Anderson, Shields Green, and Dangerfield Newby.

****

Henry and Ailsie had settled in the northwestern corner of Culpeper, an area known as "uppercutter country." Their self-sufficient farm (not productive enough to be called a plantation) was, just as others in the sparsely populated neighborhoods of the uppercutter country, dependent on slave labor.

Dangerfield was the first of Henry and Ailsie's 11 children. And since his mother was still technically the property of John Fox as of his birth, Dangerfield (and all his siblings) were born the property of John Fox as well.

I try to consider the dynamics between Ailsie's ostensibly affable owner and her common-law husband. My grandmother's stories were trimmed with a familial unity that led a listener to believe that the family lived in relative peace, yet Dangerfield and his siblings grew up laboring either on their own farm or as leased help on neighboring plantations. The Newbys' land had about 150 improved acres, with work horses, milk cows, cattle, swine, and 14 sheep the children (presumably Henry and Ailsie's children, and in time, those children's children as well) sheared for wool. They grew Indian corn and wheat. And between all that, they were rented out to work on farms around the counties.

The neighboring slave-managed lands must have been replete with families that looked like the Newbys. They must have built communities to protect the clandestine partnerships that produced children with loose ringlets, deep beige skin, broad noses and pillowy lips, who looked like both and neither parent, whose very presence was at once highly criminal and decidedly valuable.

These neighborhoods were strewn throughout the foothills of the Blue Ridge Mountains, in a region particularly fond of and influenced by "camp meetings," or what we might call church service. Protestants imported an evangelical branch of Christianity from Britain that had a considerable presence in the uppercutter freeholds of Culpeper.

Those camp churches have long since surrendered themselves to the elements, their records lost to time, but it's not preposterous to consider that Henry, or perhaps the entire family, was maybe devout. Perhaps they found a compassionate community in those camp meetings; perhaps they found safety.

In those small religious communities, John Brown was already known and his cause already embraced. He was imbued with the divine, he was prayed for. To his detractors, he was a religious fundamentalist. To his followers, he was animated by a God-given purpose, a new Moses. He would lead these people to a promised land.

As an adult, I'm apathetic about religion, but I *was* raised under my grandmother's evangelical wings. Those lessons linger a lifetime, for better or for worse. I've seen the power of my prayers, but in conversation I call it meditation and manifesting. I've felt the holy spirit swell in my chest when the entire karaoke bar erupts into a chorus together, and I've called it drunken camaraderie. I understand a force greater than any one person is connecting us all, but I also understand God is an invention of man. Today, when faced with a question of morality or ethics, I sometimes ask myself, "What would

Yeshua do?" I don't belong to any church, and I probably never will, but in this way I relate to the Newbys and to John Brown. Religion is an abstract touchstone, but it's a touchstone nonetheless.

Between 1826 and 1844 Ailsie Newby gave birth to ten more children, most of them in Culpeper. Ailsie still remained a part of the Fox estate, but she was known in their small foothill community as Henry's wife. Though census records show Henry Newby in possession of up to 21 slaves, by 1860, the Newby family all but disappeared from Virginia. In the preceding decade, a few Newbys of working age that had built families in the area, including Dangerfield, lingered in Culpeper as freed Black people, though now with manumission papers from the state of Ohio.

****

In adulthood, Dangerfield was statuesque; tall and lanky, with thick curls that appeared to lay flat, but likely only after a great deal of persuasion. His shoulders were broad and his posture rigid. His nose was both wide enough to speak to an African heritage and narrow enough to pass for something altogether different, which, by all accounts, he was. Which by all accounts, I am as well.

Dangerfield Newby
Date Unknown
Library of Congress
Call number: LOT 5910, no.113

Dangerfield mastered a number of trades: he was as skilled a blacksmith and craftsman as could be found throughout Ohio and Virginia, and had a reputation as a canny and vigorous young worker. He fell in love with a house servant named Harriet. The enslaved were not allowed to marry, so in all likelihood, Dangerfield and

Harriet jumped the broom, a tradition that sidestepped the rules of the white owner-class.

Dangerfield and Harriet would unite and start a family in the same way many other enslaved Virginians did: in the margins of their persecution, during the unaccounted-for hours in the day, when masters turned their backs or the long shadows of a heavy sun obscured their silhouettes in embrace. In the societies that developed in those margins, I really hope the two of them were able to celebrate, that Harriet put flowers in her hair and wore a delicate white dress, and Dangerfield contradicted his single stiff iconic portrait with an impassioned and poetic pronouncement of vows. On their wedding night, I hope they slept together, rather than Harriet returning to the home of the man who claimed ownership over her.

His family slowly over a number of years migrated across the Ohio River to their freedom, shepherded by their father Henry, but Dangerfield received his manumission papers after establishing residency with his father in Bridgeport at the outset of their migration. Then, Dangerfield traveled back and forth between Bridgeport, Ohio and Culpeper with the intention of raising enough capital to buy the freedom of his wife and family. Buying the freedom of your family was not an uncommon practice as more and more enslaved peoples were freed across the Ohio River. Dangerfield and

Harriet's love letters back and forth immortalized an unimaginable struggle. These letters are why my grandmother, as well as historians studying John Brown, clung so fiercely to the idea that Dangerfield followed Brown into Harpers Ferry to liberate his family.

BRENTVILLE April 11 1859

*Dear Husband I mus now write you apology for not
writing you before this but I know you will excuse me
when tell you Mrs. gennings has been very sick she has a
baby a little girl ben a grate sufferer her breast raised
and she has had it lanced and I have had to stay with
her day and night so you know I had no time to write
but she is now better and one of her own servent is now
sick I am well that is of the grates importance to you I
have no newes to write you only the chrilderen are all well
I want to see you very much but are looking fordard to
the promest time of your coming oh Dear Dangerfield
com this fall with out fail monny or no money I want to
see you so much that is one bright hope I have before me
nothing more at present but remain*

your affectionate wife HARRIETT NEWBY

P S write soon if you please

Harriet was the property of Dr. Lewis Augustine
Jennings, and was the dedicated caregiver to his wife and
newborn daughter. Because of this, Harriet was both of
particular value to Dr. Jennings, and the target of scorn
from other slaves. On a number of occasions, Dangerfield
and Dr. Jennings agreed to a price in order for

Dangerfield to purchase his family, only to have Dr. Jennings refigure the amount in the 11th hour, or increase the price after Dangerfield had presented the payment in full.

This is a frustration I cannot bend my mind enough to really imagine.

BRENTVILLE April 22 1859

Dear Husband I received your letter to day and it give much pleasure to here from you but was sorry to - -- of your sickeness hope you may be well when you receive this I wrote to you several weeks a go and directed my letter to Bridge Port but I fear you did not receive it as you said nothing about it in yours you must give my love to Brother Gabial and tell him I would like to see him very much I wrote in my last letter that Miss Virginia had a baby a little girl I had to nerse her day and night Dear Dangerfield you Can not amagine how much I want to see you Com as soon as you can for nothing would give more pleasure than to see you it is the grates Comfort I have is thinking of the promist time when you will be here oh that bless hour when I shall see you once more my baby commenced to Crall to day it is very dellicate nothing more at present but remain your affectionate wife. HARRIET NEWBY
P s write soon

My grandmother was resolute in her version of Dangerfield's story, that Dangerfield's alliance with John Brown was born from his pursuit of capital in order to buy the freedom of his wife. To hear my grandmother tell it, a true, rare love was the driving force behind his actions.

But it feels so one dimensional to assert Dangerfield's motives as lovelorn alone. If Henry and Ailsie raised their children with the same evangelical values that inspired John Brown to relentlessly pursue radical abolition, it's far more fair to assume that Dangerfield's motives were bigger than love and family. The bodies they occupied would always be of far more value than any one of them could conceivably raise. At a certain point, Dangerfield must have known that Dr. Jennings would never relinquish Harriet to him, no matter the price. But rescuing Harriet on horseback, emboldened by an army of armed, free people – this could have been what Dangerfield came to see as the only realistic route. And maybe the revolutionary plan John Brown constructed made allowances for grandiose rescues of enslaved families; maybe that was a priority that escaped the written records.

Dangerfield's bunkmates at Kennedy Farm may have described him as lovelorn. They say he shared

Harriet's letters with the company, and John Brown as well.

I think Dangerfield knew and was realistic about his odds. He knew what it meant to go to battle behind the instrument of God known as The Old Terrifyer. He knew he was Black. But also, maybe he knew that his name would be inscribed alongside John's in history, and that was his motivation. Maybe his love transcended time and place, and his actions were larger and more complex than the pursuit of freedom for his family. Maybe his actions were for his ancestors and the people who would one day call him ancestor.

In 2012, in a film written by Quentin Tarantino called *Django Unchained*, actor Jamie Foxx plays the titular Django. The story is a complex mishmash of slavery tropes, revisionism, and historical retelling, but at its core, it revolves around Django being a freed slave in want of money to buy the freedom of his wife. He joins forces with a white bounty hunter. Together, the two collect bounties until Django can afford his lover's freedom. When the film was released, I recall my grandmother's pinched face as she calmly articulated that Django's story was in fact Dangerfield's.

Django's story is rife with bloody spectacle that ends with the reunited husband and wife frolicking on horseback, a hateful plantation erupting in flames behind them. A happy ending. Dangerfield's happy endings, however, came more than a hundred years later. One of them was in the free family built by my Black grandparents.

When the movie was released, I saw it in Portland, and I could feel a theater full of white buttholes clench at every utterance of the n-word. And the script is rife with its mention. In the front of my mind, I kept my grandmother's words fresh. Dangerfield's story. And despite how bloody and brutal and cruel Django's story was, Dangerfield's was far more so; a forlorn free Black turns to a white man to help free others from bondage.

These stories already haunt the blood in my veins, they already permeate the lens through which I view the world, which is a decidedly Black thing to say, even though I'm half white. But so was Dangerfield. In every contemporary book about John Brown's raid on Harpers Ferry, Dangerfield is named as the first of the raiders to be killed, a free Black man.

But Dangerfield's compatriots described him as he was. Mixed. Just like me.

John Brown's daughter, Annie, wrote that Dangerfield was "a smart and good man for an ignorant one." Another company member called Dangerfield "a tall, well built mullato...with a pleasing face...a quiet man who never talked much about slavery and kept his intentions for joining John Brown to himself."

Of the few strands of history available to us, Dangerfield's is the thread my grandmother grasped with the most tenacity. She would really only gab about Henry and Ailsie's chilling/fairytale romance when some manner of new love cast its light on the family, but she needed no prompting to launch into the sad saga of our most newsworthy ancestor, Dangerfield. It had taken her nearly a decade of research to find him, and what she found has reverberated for generations.

Dangerfield and I share the same round, cartoonish eyes, the same slim upper lip. Our noses are wide, but not wide enough to be categorically Black. Our hair is a tangle of loose curls that are only indicative of mixed heritage to those with intimate knowledge of curl patterns. I first saw Dangerfield's picture in *Migrants Against Slavery* while my grandmother slowly died to the closing credits of *Gunsmoke* beside me. In my hands, Dangerfield's thread looked like mine.

We were always mixed. This family has always been interracial. I find purchase in Dangerfield's story, and I grasp at my Blackness, only to find it inextricably intertwined with whiteness.

a memory

Sisterhood

The morning after my first Christmas without my grandmother, I woke to a sunny, endless, blue California sky. The weather was warm, much warmer in Southern California than it was in Portland. A boy across the street was training his falcon in his driveway. I saw him once before, when my grandmother was still alive. She was visibly tickled by how dumbstruck I was seeing a boy train a falcon on the street where I grew up.

This time, I swallowed my delight. I bullied my way through my cousin and sister's houseguests on the way to dote on my son, who, with his cousin, had been tearing through the house all morning. Guests crowded the kitchen, the sitting room – wherever I wanted to be, they hovered. Rather than excusing myself, I huffed and rolled my eyes and slammed doors. For five more days at my grandmother's house, I maintained that energy.

Each time I tried to extinguish my aggression, each time I reached for a connection, I was rebuffed. When I suggested, "Let my husband watch the kids tonight and let's go have a girls night," my impromptu offer was accepted, then rudely usurped by an even more impromptu date night, as if I'd traveled here to give my sister and her husband some kind of break. Smoking weed in the backyard and coming back through the house, under-breath comments of "Ugh, you stink like weed" were made before the commenters stepped out to smoke themselves. A guest pointedly asked my son to be less...himself, and my sister echoed the sentiment without a second thought. She, I had hoped, would have established some sympathy around my son's autism by now – yet while she professed utter tolerance, this split second reaction proved otherwise.

Was I worse for guiding my son away from them, and sneering an aggressively passive comment about how annoying we must be to everyone? For spitting a venomous, drawn-out "Sorry" into their faces, my lips dripping with unaddressed acrimony?

I should have left, but the nostalgic Christmas/ New Year's holiday week, complete with the festive traditional meal and a confetti-strewn midnight revelry – a weeklong celebration of the house we'd all inherited, which I'd begun to (resentfully) call The Estate – was a commitment that kept its hand wrapped tightly around my throat.

As New Year's Eve approached, I suggested canceling the party several times over. When I found out that none of our extended family had agreed to join us, and that they had only been invited in the days after Christmas, and our aunt would be in Las Vegas, I doubled down on the cancellation.

"What are we doing? This is so much work and it seems like you didn't even, like, invite anyone or plan anything," I told my sister two nights before NYE, exasperated. She'd barely engaged our cousin in the planning, and between our cousin and myself, we'd barely invited a dozen people, which, while considerable, hardly constituted a bash of the proportions my sister seemed to desire. When confronted, my sister flopped across the couch like a Victorian damsel and whined about how much she *deserved* a party. After all she's been through, after how hard her year was. All she wanted was a party. Just one party.

I was incredulous. I asked if she'd been relying on me to invite friends I hadn't seen or talked to in the ten-plus years since I'd moved away, and she mewled again. She just wanted a party. Why didn't I understand? Why was it so wrong for her to want this one thing?

I swallowed my angst. This argument would never fly in the face of our mother or grandmother.

The reason I'd learned to play "Auld Lang Syne" was because I assumed there would be a household of family members to sing along with me as the clock struck midnight. But the piano had been buried. I walked away from the conversation in a huff, leaving my sister sprawled dramatically across the sofa and my cousin standing between us.

Later my cousin and I agreed that, despite most of our friends and family members already having plans, we'd do what we could to pull together a decent party. I called everyone I knew. The clock ticked towards 2020 and I counted the minutes.

The night before New Year's Eve, my sister confronted me. She felt justified. In her eyes, I'd been grumbling around the house with no explanation, angry at everyone. But every time I tried to talk, it became two conversations – the one I heard and the one she heard – and they were at odds every time.

I speak the language of her privilege and I hate that about myself. She doesn't speak the language of my struggle and I resent that about her.

She cornered me in what once was our grandmother's "day room," an add-on to the house that opens up onto a paved back patio lined with young bougainvillea bushes my uncle planted. My sister had claimed that room for herself as well; detritus from her creative projects littered every inch of floorspace. As usual, I couldn't articulate my anger, so I blurted something about how I shouldn't have come, and that I wasn't emotionally ready to spend a holiday in the house without Grandma. It was too crowded, I was too sensitive, Rainier's autism made me anxious around people who weren't family.

I said a lot of things, and though all of them certainly needed saying, I still couldn't explain what was twisting me up so violently.

I wanted to say that, by keeping this house as a residence after Grandmother died, we were inviting more trauma. Fights woulds ensue, relationships would crumble, someone would feel their claim somehow eclipses the claims of the other inheritors. We would crowd each other, alienate each other, and eventually destroy the love between each other, and then we would have no house, and at least one of us would think it was our greatest loss.

But no one was seeing the far greater loss of our sisterhood. That loss meant an even thinner connection to not just everything our grandparents built for us – the potential new homes and new businesses and new legacies they intended us to inherit – but also the ideals instilled in us.

My sister confessed she visited our grandmother's grave to ask for guidance in keeping our family strong and whole. I tried to imagine what Grandma would say, to call on some latent, inherited knowledge that would be a salve to this fissure, but I came up with nothing. She told me that as sisters, we were all we had, and I said, "Stop saying that. You have this house, and a whole family; stop putting all this pressure on me to be there for you all the time when you can't even meet me halfway." The phrase "we are all we have" clawed at a part of me that had been empty long enough to gather dust, so when I told her to stop saying it, my words were loaded with the unsaid. They dripped with feeling, but as they fell from my mouth, I could see how flimsy they were. I wanted her to meet me halfway but I didn't know where halfway was.

The sisterhood she pleaded for me to help her maintain is not the sisterhood I wanted. In this way, I was no better than she, sprawled across the couch dramatically crying for someone else to throw me my perfect party.

The way my sister and cousin doted on their guests to my exclusion had swollen to take up a preposterous amount of my headspace, and I was being petty. Between the two of us, I could feel the successes and failures of our mother magnified, and we were opposing poles. I was treading three feet of water. I was a betta fish fighting my own reflection. If I let us, we could be stuck in this limbo forever, petty versus righteous, righteous versus petty, volleying forever.

Outside looking in, I was hiding the heirloom of intimacy from my sister because I was pissy about a piano, a seat at the dinner table, an inhospitable, crowded house. Now it was her begging me for connection, but imploring me to be "all she had" threw me off. It was just enough to imply she was too spoiled to deserve any of my support and attention. Just enough to imply that her privilege disturbed me perhaps more than my own.

The voice in my head instigated my rancor. "She always gets everything, you always get nothing," it repeated. "She gets all the love, all the patience, all the money and designer shopping sprees and cozy weekend trips, all the opportunities to build her own wealth while you're left to forever spin your wheels."

The voice wasn't necessarily wrong, but its frame was too violently warped to be credible. I had those opportunities too. I just made different choices.

The argument petered out with us smoking joints together and apologizing for things neither of us had really unpacked or made sense of.

The next night we threw a party, lit sparklers, threw confetti, and danced. We pretended everything was fine. My husband, son, and I left before dawn the next morning.

The two-day drive back to Portland was quiet. My chest felt raw and empty. I wanted it to be years before I came back to San Pedro. I even entertained never coming back at all.

But what would that make me? Without the women in my life who built the foundations of me, what was I? Those connections were lifelines I'd taken for granted; those were the only women I could talk to about my Blackness. If no one I see acknowledges me as Black, and I disconnect even more from the family that made me so, can I still claim their power? Do I still belong to them?

My worth has been tied to my identity for all my life in this tangle of emotions and memories that I don't understand. Or that I'm just beginning to understand.

I think that my idea of worth is ineffectual. That my idea of wealth is one-dimensional. That I only perform confidence, competency, and compassion, and I don't know where performance ends and authenticity begins. It feels like I am almost too relatable, my patchwork heritage reflecting a million faces, but I've lost all the familiarity to the faces I grew up focused on. Now, I only exist through unfamiliar eyes I can't see myself through.

I spent the entire drive home silently trying to distill everything I was feeling into one cohesive thought. I was trying to compartmentalize my grief, store it away in a hidden pocket of my psyche, but its breadth defied storage.

I feel that I've let my family down in ways I can't articulate, ways I don't entirely understand myself. It's a cacophony of emotions too chaotic to unpack, but one opinion resonates stronger and louder than the rest. In the wake of these matriarchal deaths and shifts and fissures, I am wondering for the first time in my life whether or not my ancestors know my name.

I wonder whether they should.

The Raid

As Kennedy Farm welcomed Kansas abolitionists, Brown's daughter, Annie, was tasked with intercepting meddlesome neighbors inquiring about the farm's seemingly endless stream of guests. She was devoted to Brown's growing army. She called them her "invisibles."

How sequestered must one company be to be nicknamed "invisible"?

Dangerfield stayed on Brown's farm for a considerable amount of time. Osborne Perry Anderson's notes on the stay, which would become the memoir *A Voice From Harper's Ferry*, detail a confinement that primarily sequestered men in the log cabin's attic as they planned their attack.

Anderson was born free in 1830. He attended Oberlin College in Ohio, at the time a radical institution (the campus both was multi-racial and co-ed) that was founded on the same abolitionist Christian motives that drove John Brown. After completing his schooling, Anderson moved to Chatham, or what is now known as

Ontario, Canada, at the terminus of the Underground Railroad. He opened a print shop there; he also served as a member of the Chatham Vigilance Committee, a group that fought to protect enslaved persons who had escaped to Canada from interloping slave catchers/bounty hunters. It was there in Chatham that Anderson reportedly first met John Brown and learned of his plan to raid Harpers Ferry.

I pore over Osborne Perry Anderson's writings and wonder if Dangerfield kept a journal of his time at Kennedy Farm as well. Perhaps, rather than a journal, his time was encapsulated in letters to Harriet. My insides squirm at the thought of this houseful of men, quietly and secretly planning an insurrection that would reverberate through history, crowded in the attic of a cabin, their breath hanging in thick air, sweat curling the hairs on the backs of their necks. Training to use one shot for one kill while their hearts thumped for wives and children and partners and mothers they must have known they may never see again.

Months ticked down to weeks and weeks to days as these men steeled themselves to march behind The Old Terrifyer, to become the defining spark of an uncontainable blaze.

After George Floyd was murdered by police in May of 2020, I avoided every protest that snaked through my neighborhood. I was terrified of Portland's powers that be, terrified of unhinged officers who snatched people off the streets and disappeared them in windowless black vans, terrified of rural "Oregunians" who convoyed their lifted trucks through our quadrant of the city – the quadrant historically occupied by Black families – AR15 rifles pointed to the sky. That fear always felt rational, but when I try to contextualize my skittish behavior in response to justice paralleled to Dangerfield, I wonder if I'm carrying fears and anxieties my ancestors hoped I'd never have, that they sacrificed their lives to prevent me from carrying. What is cowardice and what is bravery, and why are the lines between them so finely drawn? When is self-preservation braver than sacrifice? Is it ever?

In *A Voice From Harper's Ferry*, Anderson notes,

> "When our resources became pretty well exhausted, the ennui from confinement, imposed silence, etc., would make the men almost desperate. At such times, neither slavery nor slaveholders were discussed mincingly. We were, while the ladies remained, often relieved of the dullness growing out of restraint by their kindness."

In those snatched moments of raw masculine vulnerability, what did Dangerfield say about John Fox and the prodigious Fox estate, and what did he say about his mother and father and sisters and brothers, and his wife and children? What was he like when all his defenses were down? Did he weep without grimacing, the way my mother sometimes did? Did he laugh so hard he wheezed and buckled, like I do? What did he look like when his face was twisted in emotion? While the raiders planned and trained and ate and slept at the farmhouse, no less than four enslaved people died on surrounding farms. Three were murdered as punishment. One hung themselves after learning they would be sold south. Was space left in the attic for grieving, or did the men put their feelings aside until they could feel in private?

In addition to two overstuffed binders, I brought three of my grandmother's books on Harpers Ferry home with me from her wake. One was a children's book titled *The Story of John Brown's Raid on Harpers Ferry,* by Zachary Kent. The book told a concise, if editorialized, version of the raid, illustrated and sanitized for grade school. It was from a collection called *Cornerstones of Freedom,* published by Children's Press. A painted portrait of John Brown was the cover.

Another book I absconded with was *The Raid* by Laurence Greene. Published in 1953, it aimed to memorialize the raid through the eyes of the victim residents of Harpers Ferry. *The Raid* was written like a novel, with imagined conversations and emotions built around the written history of the event.

The third book was *Migrants Against Slavery*.

In each book, Dangerfield joins John Brown's raiding party in want of money to free his enslaved wife. Each book pulls quotes from Harriet's letters. Three white writers, six white lenses, but between the three tomes, I could begin to conceptualize the events that led to Dangerfield's death. But It was Osborne Perry Anderson's *A Voice From Harper's Ferry*, my own first Harpers Ferry book purchase, that brought me nearest to Dangerfield.

Osborne Perry Anderson describes Dangerfield as his comrade, and I think I feel a certain tenderness in Anderson's portrayal. His impassioned memoir of the incident at Harpers Ferry is as close as I'll get to hearing Dangerfield describe it himself. Osborne was the sole survivor of the raid. Reading his story feels like being in the same room with Dangerfield, but only catching glimpses of him. The feeling is bittersweet; this is as close as I will ever be to him.

****

On the morning of October 16th, 1859, John Brown rose earlier than usual and called his men down from their bunks to pray. By that afternoon, 11 orders were presented. The orders detailed positions and actions the men would take (like the tearing down of telegraph wires), when to use iron pikes Brown had provided and when to use their rifles, and which prisoner would be taken first and hand off their arms to the free Osborne after capture for peak poetic value (it was the nephew of George Washington). In the evening, when all the preparations were secured, John Brown's party marched two by two towards the small town of Harpers Ferry.

The men were given the order to take two prisoners of significance, and invite those enslaved by those prisoners and any free Blacks they met along the way to come and stand with them at the Armory. First they took Lewis Washington prisoner, George's nephew. Osborne describes taking Washington, and notes that he offered up his slaves first: "You can have my slaves, if you will let me remain." As if, in the moment, the choice was his to make. He "blubbered" when he realized he must submit.

I relish that.

The second slave owner taken on the parade towards Harpers Ferry was John Allstat. His seven male slaves joined their party.

Murmurs of Johns Brown's plan to lead an uprising had already been swirling. The town had now begun to hum.

When the first two raiders approached the covered Potomac River Bridge, each holding two pistols and a rifle underneath their wool cloaks, there was one watchman stationed at the bridge. They took him prisoner.

The night was clear and cool, the damp edge of autumn permeating the evening atmosphere with a chill that suspended the mist from the river as if it was a light rain. Every book I've read about this event mentions the damp October air, and with each mention I'm reminded of my birthday. All the birthdays, all the autumn chills, all the evenings that twinkle with suspended mist.

After the Potomac Bridge was taken, the articles of Brown's plan fell neatly into place. The town offered little resistance. Guards and watchmen surrendered through sloppy, tearful pleadings. At the engine house near the mouth of the Armory, a watchman locked himself behind the gate and wailed for mercy. The men forced the gates open to take him prisoner. The men told the guard their intention was to free the slaves, and their prisoners would only have to submit until that purpose was carried out. They had no intention to harm.

John Brown trailed his party in a one-horse wagon as they crossed the now-taken bridge. Two more raiders would hold sentinel, using pikes John Brown had collected. Before the raid, Brown declared to his company that they should not take the life of anyone if they could possibly avoid it. But if it was necessary, "then to make sure work of it."

During the raid, Brown addressed his captives, saying "I came here from Kansas, and this is a slave state. I want to free all the negroes. I seek possession of the US Armory, and if the citizens interfere with me I must only burn the town and have blood." When then the party marched through the town square, past the train depot and the Wagner House Hotel, and onwards towards the stark, looming towers of the arsenal buildings, they were presumably several bodies deep. Brown ordered Anderson to start handing out the iron pikes he had stowed in the wagon.

Once through the arsenal gate, the party captured another watchman and headquartered themselves in a brick storehouse built for fire fighting equipment. John then sent four party members into the streets of Harpers Ferry to raid a rifle works a few blocks down the street.

Even though I've read through the timeline events many times over, I still like to imagine Dangerfield entering Colonel Washington's house alongside Anderson. I imagine him nodding in silence to stunned house servants doing nightly chores before snatching the thunderstruck Washington from an austere four-poster bed by gunpoint. In my mind's eye, I can see him herding his white captives through the streets of Harpers Ferry, bullying them through the gates of the Armory, and forcing them into the mouth of an impending war. I see him emboldening people along the way to join the crusade and returning to the arsenal 10, 20, 30 men stronger than he left.

Other times I imagine him as John Brown's solemn protector, a confident sure shot with a steely gaze and captivating, quiet intensity. In those imagined scenarios, I see Dangerfield's stoic mask crack only when his face is turned away from Brown. In those moments I see his face twisted in grief, reliving the loss of his family again and again. And when he sobs, I imagine his face looks like mine, our outbursts of emotion staying similarly hidden until they can no longer be concealed.

****

At midnight, a passenger train approached the second bridge over the Potomac. The conductor stopped the train at the sight of the men blocking entry. A baggage handler/ticket seller on the Maryland side of the train tracks came out to investigate. He was ordered to halt by John's men. Maybe he heard them, maybe he didn't. He proceeded to approach and he was shot. He died the next day, the first known casualty of the raid. His name was Hayward Shepard and he was a free Black man.

The first to die as a result of the raid was a Black man, The first raider to die was a Black man. I can't help but wonder what Hayward Shepherd was mixed with. His death was proselytized to be the reason the raid didn't erupt into a volcanic uprising, but Anderson's memoir attests that the raiders did not, could not, have known the race of Shepherd.

In the meantime, John Brown's followers returned to the headquarters with hostages, household weapons they'd gathered, and a small number of enslaved persons.

As the night wore on, Brown's men captured more than 40 people. And quickly, citizens were compelled to either escape what would surely be a bloody battle, or answer a call to arms and rush into the conflict. The streets grew rowdy with rumors of insurrection so great they eclipsed the truer terror of the conflict: white panic.

Satisfied his raid was gaining momentum while remaining peaceful, Brown sent word back to Kennedy Farm of the night's success. As the message moved through the countryside, armed militias began to crowd the streets.

The next morning, Brown granted passage to the train halted at the second river bridge. Allowing them passage was a tactic to show clemency. To prove to the watching world that he meant no harm, that he and his raiders had come to free the enslaved, not murder congregating countrymen. The horror was the militias, storming into the town to kill for the right to kill.

When the train reached the next station, where, incidentally, the telegraph wires had not been cut, the conductor relayed a distressed message to townships in all directions:

"AN INSURRECTION HAS BROKEN OUT AT HARPERS FERRY WHERE AN ARMED BAND OF ABOLITIONISTS HAVE FULL POSSESSION OF THE GOVERNMENT ARSENAL AND THE TOWN. THE INSURRECTIONISTS SAY THEY HAVE COME TO FREE THE SLAVES AND INTEND TO DO IT AT ALL HAZARDS"

Even more pro-slave Marylanders and Virginians heeded the call and convened upon Harpers Ferry, drunk with entitlement, their guns drawn. Hundreds of them gathered facing the armory, chanting "Kill Them! Kill Them!" A local militia seized back control of the bridges, and before the clock tower in the town square had struck noon on October 17th, the armory had erupted in gunfire.

Dangerfield had been stationed at the Shenandoah Bridge. In the cool night, before the needle tipped, before the penny dropped, before the tide turned against them, I hope he felt both terror and rapture; which is to say, I hope he felt wholly justified taking hostages, and at peace with sacrificing his life, a sacrifice he must have realized by now was likely a requisite. If he held on to the grandiose hope of rescuing Harriet and the children with John's one-horse wagon, maybe setting the

Jennings estate ablaze before riding back to Bridgeport to rejoin his mother and father with his own family, I hope it kept him brave but also kept him kind.

Osborne Perry Anderson watched as Dangerfield became the first of the company to take a fatal shot. Besieged, approaching the security of the engine house, Dangerfield was shot in the neck not by a bullet, but by a six-inch iron spike fired from a gun. The spike slashed his throat from ear to ear. Citizens emboldened by the weakening forces of Brown milled around Dangerfield's body, mutilating and dismembering him. Stealing his flesh for souvenirs.

Perhaps this is why a fear of armed white people emboldened by a status quo that represses and marginalizes me, but uplifts and comforts them, is coded into my DNA. Perhaps this is why I fear convoys of Oregunians, and blue walls of police officers holding riot shields, always ready to foment chaos on the wrong side of history.

Osowatomie Brown's party had been overtaken. John was then arrested, convicted of treason, and in the weeks that followed, executed by hanging.

The bodies of the dead, including Dangerfield, lay on the battlefield for three days. When his desecrated corpse was finally collected, a letter from Harriet was found in his coat pocket. It read:

BRENTVILLE, August 16, 1859.

Dear Husband.

Your kind letter came duly to hand and it gave me much pleasure to here from you and especely to hear you are better of your rhumatism and hope when I here from you again you may be entirely well. I want you to buy me as soon as possible for if you do not get me somebody else will the servents are very disagreeable thay do all thay can to set my mistress againt me Dear Husband you not the trouble I see the last two years has ben like a trouble dream to me it is said Master is in want of monney if so I know not what time he may sell me an then all my bright hops of the futer are blasted for there has ben one bright hope to cheer me in all my troubles that is to be with you for if I thought I shoul never see you this earth would have no charms for me do all you Can for me witch I have no doubt you will I want to see you so much the Chrildren are all well the baby cannot walk yet all it can step around enny thing by holding on it is very much like Agnes I mus bring my letter to Close as I have no newes to write you mus write soon and say when you think you Can Come.

Your affectionate Wife
HARRIET NEWBY.

John Brown's raid on Harpers Ferry failed in its immediate aims, but the act was not a failure. The event initiated a civil war that would eventually see abolition, but the party fell in the battle, and John Brown was hung for treason. The sole survivor, Osborne Perry Anderson escaped to Canada through the underground railroad, but returned to the US to fight in the Civil War, recruit free Blacks to the Union cause, and raise money in order to publish *A Voice From Harpers Ferry*, which he wrote as a fugitive. Impoverished, he succumbed to tuberculosis in 1872

For over a century, Dangerfield's name was almost never mentioned in histories of Harpers Ferry. And in more recent texts, it's included exclusively in relation to John Brown, always with a letter from Harriet, and he's always referred to as the first of the Harpers Ferry raiders to die in battle. A free, Black man.

But Dangerfield was mixed like me. The more I learn about him, the more I want to rectify his two dimensional portrayal as John Brown's first sacrificial lamb. The more I learn, the more I wish my grandmother was here to sift through all these notes with me, to guide me through her own pages, to make the new ones feel more familiar. I feel Dangerfield's presence in her absence. I wouldn't be here, sketching pictures of how I imagine him with his family, organizing a timeline of his short life, comparing my reluctance to embrace my history with history's reluctance to embrace Dangerfield, Osborne, Shields Green, Lewis Leary, and John Copeland – the five Black raiders of Harpers Ferry – if I hadn't lost my mother and grandmother the way I did. If I hadn't become so untethered in the first place, Dangerfield's death may never have become a lifeline.

Perhaps identity is mercurial. Perhaps it can be reframed and redrawn like history, through the lens of a storyteller. The stories my grandmother tells. The stories historians tell. The story Osborne Perry told. What truths are missing from these accounts, and if I ever found them, how would my own frame of reference color them?

What story did Dangerfield tell about himself?

He appealed to two of his brothers, Gabriel and James, to join the Harpers Ferry raid, but never told them why. And they never came. Unlike most of the company who remained sequestered in the weeks before the raid, Dangerfield came and went as he pleased, working on a farm along the border. Brown's daughter, I suspect, had a crush on him. She described him as a "splendid light skinned specimen." But for all the superficial descriptions, what do any of us know about Dangerfield?

He loved his wife and children and ached for their freedom. He died fighting to free them. Perhaps my worth cannot, and should not, be tied to my ancestry. Dangerfield didn't die for me, but maybe he died for the idea of me. And for the idea of my mother, who would improve the lives of thousands of children, and the idea of my grandmother, who would spend a lifetime in service to her culture, to the family that she traced back to Dangerfield, Harriet, Ailsie, and Henry. I could spend a lifetime asking myself where my own superficial ideas of worth end and where my own identity begins. But it wouldn't matter. Someone else could reinterpret my words and actions in a hundred years and render it all for nothing.

One generation plants roses, the next tears them up.

The tether that holds me to Dangerfield is that I'm alive because of him. His story can be reframed a thousand times, but maybe my frame is important too. Our shared heritage, our mixed blood, our life between the rock of whiteness and the hard place of Blackness – we share these things. My grandma knew this. She put these stories in my hands for a reason.

I'm not the steward of a trust, a house in the suburbs, an antique parlor piano, or the flowers planted in someone else's garden. I am the steward of my story, and my story is woven from the threads of mothers and sons and daughters and sisters and friends who left fragments of lives that I might better understand when my own interpretations are unfettered by anyone else's perspective. I'm the steward of a singular lens through which to see my place in history. This is the heirloom.

Whatever valuables that came with this birthright, I've already inherited.

Consequences of Ownership

A few weeks after returning to Portland from that first holiday without Grandma, I received a heavy manila envelope from my uncle in the mail. Inside was a copy of my grandmother's last will and testament, along with a certified letter declaring an intention to sue over the fine print of my grandmother's trust.

My aunt, sister, cousin, and I were the defendants. The complaint was that the home should be sold immediately, and any contents left by the deceased liquidated. Worse than whittling our legacy down to zeros in a bank account, the suit was pitting the residents against each other while keeping them in a perpetual holding pattern. People lived there, a child was being raised there. No one was just going to agree and leave without a fight.

Well, except me. I'd already left.

During our initial post-mortem meeting with the law firm who wrote our grandparents' trust, fresh off the heels of our grandmother's death, I had opted to sell my ownership of the house back to my cousin. My cousin told me she would sooner buy my share than sell the whole house. So without considering out loud how she could possibly afford my share or what that might mean for her in the long run I said, "Bet."

My sister waffled. She wanted to sell her share to our cousin as well, but under a vague caveat that also allowed her and her growing family to live there as long as they wanted.

The estate's worth was substantial, even when split among us. It was a dramatic amount of liquid cash, plus a simple tract house in suburban Los Angeles. Just out of earshot of the massive port, an ocean breeze forever rippling endless lanes of palm, lemon, and jacaranda trees. Seventy-eight degrees all year.

I didn't want the financial confusion of partly owning her home, but even more than potential financial responsibilities, and regardless of anyone's inherited, generational feelings, this house had come to represent distress in my life. Everyone who now lived beneath its roof seemed wholly dedicated to perpetuating that energy. And I would be expected to rally alongside them, supporting a fight I'd made deliberate moves to avoid.

The stink of the holiday still in my mouth, I reached out to my sister, cousin, and aunt to see how everyone was reacting to my uncle's lawsuit. My cousin, the daughter of the plaintiff, was resolute. She wanted the house, she wanted to preserve some type of residential legacy, she wanted to die there. My best judgment told me to resist and to encourage the sale of the house; it was a testimony that had been brewing in me, to convince the residents of what they were giving up to live there. A childhood sanctuary had been conflated with a suburban tract home, but this house was not my home, and the only argument I could realistically make felt like an echo of my uncle. I couldn't relate, so as usual, I kept my mouth shut.

My sister and her husband reiterated through tight lips and furrowed brows they would relocate as soon as possible, their puckered faces obfuscating their reluctance to admit that they would likely live there years past their self-imposed expiration date.

My cousin alone wanted to own the house. Three bedrooms, a family room, a two-car garage, a sunroom, a backyard built for big family cookouts and birthday parties, a wide open living room with a stone fireplace that reddened the cheeks of an entire family every Christmas. For only one person, it felt like maybe more of an albatross than an extravagant birthright. But of the three of us, my cousin was the most emotionally invested in the home, and though my sister's connection with my grandmother was incandescent and undeniable, I often thought of my cousin as my grandma's best friend. I didn't agree with her reasoning for wanting to keep the house for herself, but I understood it. Through her framework, shoes needed to be filled, and as the first-born grandchild, she should be the one to fill them.

In the deeper parts of myself, the parts I'd rather not recognize, I desperately wanted to argue them into homes of their own. I wanted to contact a lawyer and use my inflated percentage to force a sale. I wanted to see what each of them would do without the safety net they knew, with only their own devices and the outrageous advantage of six unearned digits in their bank accounts.

Maybe it was because of how the house made me feel. Every time I crossed the threshold, the weight of my mother's legacy, of my failure to meet the challenge of her excellence, crushed me. I felt the crisscrossing antagonism of greed and grief that had possessed all who laid claim to the estate.

And every time I returned, I felt the wounds of my escape. Without recourse, I fell into the role of veiled victim freely, smiling when complimented on my patience, my supportiveness, and my strength.

In his lawsuit, my uncle pointed to his perceived value of the house he grew up in. The house where he planted flowers, laid stonework, and, in his mind, cared for his ailing mother. By his estimation, this suburban tract house, one of many in a neatly divided grid between the dueling skylines of refinery smokestacks and skeletal shipping cranes, was worth nearly a million dollars, and he intended to not only evict each remaining resident, but also collect retroactive rent from their remaining shares of the trust. Despite disappearing from the house after my grandmother's funeral, leaving behind decades of ephemera stored in the deepest corners of the garage, he asserted he was entitled to thousands of dollars in payments from his erstwhile housemates.

Barely a year had passed since Grandma had died, and even with the months she spent planning for her mortality, the process of closing her accounts was categorically time consuming. My aunt, my grandmother's youngest child, took it all on alone. There was nothing I could do from Portland, but even if I could, what would I have wanted to do? The impotence, resentment, and simmering bitterness I'd refined over the last year of grief was honing itself into a blade, and I could feel the edge of it tighten against my throat with each mention of the estate.

I would now have to navigate this lawsuit with a family that couldn't have bothered to save me a seat at the Christmas dinner table for a meal that I had cooked.

I was so full of a resentment, but so much of it shouldn't have even belonged to me. I want to give it back, but who would I give it back to? Dead people?

Speaking with my cousin after studying the lawsuit, I advocate to have the plaintiff removed from the trust completely. I fantasize about how much larger that might make my share, but I keep that to myself. Even though I promised my share of the house to my cousin, I feel certain that she simply cannot afford it, but her finances are "none of my business." So rather than initiate a discussion, I vent to my friends. They insist I get a lawyer of my own, that my interests are so dissimilar to my aunt's, sister's, and cousin's that I must find representation. I promised I would, but frankly, I wasn't sure what my interests were.

Eventually I did reach out to a lawyer, a friend of a friend of a friend. The lawyer advised me to exercise my larger shares to push for the sale of the house straightaway. Slam dunk, easy. Boilerplate advice for a boilerplate family dispute. She told me she handles cases just like this all the time. I asked her if families ever spend years arguing over estates. "Oh yeah," she said, "trusts are consistently disputed. It can be sad."

She said "it can be sad" very casually, as if to punctuate the thought with a shrug and a hair flip, and I wondered if she was numb to watching families collapse. I started to ask her more about it, but she steered me back to my options as an inheritor. I was resistant to legal representation, but vague about why. I already knew I wouldn't hire her. I wouldn't try to evict my family from their home or take them to court over percentages, nickels and dimes. In the lawyer's estimation, I was being taken advantage of; the residents could at least pay me rent, since according to the fine print of the trust, the house was to be made productive (ie: rented out) if it wasn't sold.

I'd already heard it, and talking to her just felt like a due diligence I was performing. I'd already paid for the consultation, I was bored of unpacking the arduous details of the case, so instead I began to download all the tumultuous, corrosive emotions I was experiencing.

Her hourly rate was twice that of my therapist. Was I justified?

I described to this stranger our family dynamic at length. I narrated the opaque turmoil between my mother and her siblings. I reminisced about my grandmother as some kind of otherworldly matriarch. I speculated about how my mother would have handled executing the estate if she were still alive. I thought she would have been messy but capable, and everything still would have come together the same way. Someone contesting something. I whined about how spoiled entitlement would always make an appearance to remind everyone how disconnected we are from our legacy.

At some point I began to exploit the therapeutic vibe I'd foisted upon the lawyer. I described the heartbreak of seeing my piano packed away so thoughtlessly, and the hair-raising discomfort of watching the dynamics of the house shift and curdle as my sister and cousin tried to establish dominance. I reminisced about my grandmother's paperback Louis L'Amour collection, and I lamented not snatching a few editions for my own collection.

I explained how I was reliving every sadness of my childhood because with death comes way too many foundational shifts and crashes and undoings. I confessed how exhausted I was at being described as brave or stoic or strong, how it felt like I was drowning, begging for someone's hand, and just getting a bunch of high fives instead. I professed that I was remembering sadness in a way that excluded my adolescence, which I know was, comparatively, joyful and free. I explained how the sticky midpoint between Blackness and whiteness and gayness and now disability that I stayed snarled in, for better or worse, threaded every corner of my life. I told her I felt untethered since my mother's death, and now that my grandma was gone, I was lost at sea. I admitted that I needed them, but my family was too wrapped in their own sticky threads to see me.

I told her I felt like I was letting down my ancestors, and I asked her, since she handled cases like this so frequently, if she had some insight as to why, but then I barreled through her answer.

I told her since it was probably my fault my mom died, maybe I shouldn't get anything at all.

I was starting to choke up. Rather than fight it as I usually would, I let out a big wet sob.

The other end of the phone went quiet as I gushed and gasped and stuttered an apology.

"It's totally fine," she said, with velvety condolence in her voice.

Of course it was fine. She handled cases like this all the time.

****

The opportunity to push my sister and cousin out of the nest just because I couldn't find space for myself was petty. Any one of us could have presented a lawyer with the same scenario, from a different perspective, and they still would have gotten some variation of advice that would fracture my family in ways that would break my grandmother's heart.

I started to tell the lawyer that I didn't really have any intention to take anyone to court, but my voice was pure mist. I exhaled the words "I don't want to..." and then I paused. I took a steadying breath and remembered my sister and me playing in an empty refrigerator box on the front lawn of the house a few years before the rose bushes were planted, sometime in the early '90s. The yard was thick with neatly trimmed, hyper-green grass. Each house on the block was neater than the next. We pretended the box was our secret clubhouse that led to outer space, and when we slept that night in bedrooms across the hall from one another, I had a nightmare that she got lost in the deep black end of the refrigerator box. I was terrified, devastated, convinced it was my fault and that my sister had perished because of me. Because of something I had done. I woke myself up crying. The nightmare haunted me for years, even into adulthood. My sister was the most important thing in the world to me when we were children, playing on the front lawn of the house that now stood between us.

The memory evaporated and I croaked, "you know, last year I cooked their entire Christmas dinner and they didn't even save a place for me at the table. Isn't that so fucked up? Fucking jerks. Tell me, what would you do?"

In that velvety tone, the lawyer explained that it wouldn't happen to her. She handled cases like this all the time; she's learned a few things about watertight wills.

Later that evening, I reflected on how I so quickly confessed my regrets and resentments to a featureless lawyer but couldn't compel myself to share those thoughts with the family members who probably needed to hear me as much as I needed to be heard.

A final thread began to unravel inside me. I resented the ease with which those whose potential was not a burden seemed to move through the world. I resented the world for taking all my mothers. I resented all my mothers for looking nothing like me until they looked exactly like me. I resented them for dying before we got the chance to gaze into mirrors, side by side, appreciating the similarities. I resented myself for resenting anything. And all the resentment had been honed to a blade, and perhaps, if I hadn't called a lawyer on that day, I wouldn't have felt that overwhelming rush of resentment slice my throat clean in half.

****

Near the end of her life, Grandma needed blood transfusions every week. During my last visit, all three granddaughters accompanied her to the lab for her transfusion.

The tech was amused by our charming camaraderie. As he slipped a needle into my grandmother's waiting arm, she made a darling comment, something about how we were her squad and accompanied her to all her appointments. We were her little entourage.

My sister and cousin broke into a choreographed dance they had been practicing together and I stood to the side, equal parts amused and excluded.

My grandmother giggled as the blood in her veins, the blood that made us the family that we are, was slowly diluted, and I wondered what it meant that the blood was still flowing through mine. I looked at the blue veins in my own arm, and saw that my grandmother and I were almost the same shade of beige-y yellow. She was at her palest. Our wrists were the color of custard. What was simmering under the surface of this buttersoft skin, and why was I so galvanized with the feeling?

Our blood was speaking to me then. I couldn't make out the words, but I could feel their resonance, anchoring me in an intangible feeling of home.

Reintroduction

Dangerfield's story did not end at Harpers Ferry. His family still had to learn of his death, about the raid, about Harriet being sold, and what all these changes would mean for their own futures.

The news of Dangerfield's death reached his mother Ailsie around the same time as did the news of her former master John Fox's last will and testament, executed by the groundskeeper of the Fox estate, Eli Tackett.

John Fox, Ailsie's affable, longtime owner, died the same year as her first-born son. Fox's estate, as was his wish, was to be dispersed to all those he enslaved.

The recurrence of Eli Tackett's name in reference to the Fox estate broke a dam of emotional questions for me. How intimately did Eli and Ailsie know each other? Were they close in age or was Eli purchased after Ailsie had been given away? Did one perform the functions of an older sibling to the other, or were they close enough in age for the gap to disappear? Did they have a shared history – did traces of Eli's blood flow through Aislie's veins? And does Eli's blood flow through mine?

I like to imagine Eli and Aislie grew up together, and were close enough in age that, when reunited, there were celebratory emotions in the air. I imagine them having a sibling-esque relationship that maybe simmered in petty animosities or grumbly grievances, but was primarily a relationship built from the enduring attachment between brothers and sisters. I imagine Eli might have missed Ailsie terribly when she left the Fox estate on the arm of Henry Newby, but I also imagine Eli knew that velvet ropes were preferable to shackles.

Sifting through the piecemeal documents of my grandmother's collection, I eventually discerned that Eli Tackett, the once and future groundskeeper of the Fox estate, had married Ailsie's oldest granddaughter: Dangerfield and Harriet's eldest daughter, Elmira, named for Dangerfield's sister. After the death of Dangerfield, Elmira's mother and siblings had been sold "down the river" to Louisiana. Save for a few aunts and uncles in the area, the 14-year-old Elmira (or "Mira" as she was nicknamed) was left in Virginia to fend for herself.

Eli was 23 years her senior when he took her as a teenage bride. Their first son was named James. They would parent three more children before parting ways. Before his death, John Fox had allocated $30,000 to free and relocate any of his slaves who wished to migrate to

Bridgeport, but more than that, he intended to leave the entirety of the Virginia estate to his remaining living slaves. And so Eli had traveled from Virginia to Ohio to let his veritable mother-in-law know that technically, as Ailsie was still the property of John Fox, Ailsie was included in the inheritance.

John Fox had no recorded living heirs, because white heirs born from legal matrimony were the only heirs officially recorded. However, John had many unrecorded heirs, and in drafting this will, he concerned himself with their well-being, rather than the monetary opportunities the estate would provide for his last remaining sibling's family.

The years between the death of Sam Fox, the institutionalization of James Fox, and this drafting of John Fox's last will and testament had seen John become one of the most prodigious landowners in the state, both his human chattel and his acres so numerous they defied estimation and required diligent detailed accounting.

By 1858, John Fox's health was failing. He had spent the preceding years, in anticipation of his growing frailty, traveling north to free states, searching for somewhere those he had enslaved could settle after his passing. His intention was for them all to be freed after his death, and that those that did not wish to migrate should inherit the estate which they had dedicated their lives to.

It seems like John purposefully excluded everyone but those he enslaved from his will. And this was a decision his estranged sibling's family was prepared to fight.

While no one had been explicitly written out of my grandmother's will, an amendment made after my sister and her family moved in that allowed for unlimited residence by inheritors certainly seemed to muddy her intentions in a similar way. I suppose it is the curse of the well-intentioned estate, to be disputed and argued and dissected in perpetuity, because even the best intentions can not satisfy everyone.

Any estate lawyer can tell you that. They handle cases like this all the time.

****

Dolly Ferguson, John's estranged half-sister and daughter of Sam Fox, who unsuccessfully attempted to argue her inclusion into his will and subsequently became untangled from the Fox family entirely, had indoctrinated her children so thoroughly that when the rumors of what would become of the Fox estate reached their own homes, they'd already been prepared to fight for a share of the inheritance. They had been waiting for this moment their whole lives –the death of John Fox and their perceived rightful claim to the Fox fortune.

John Fox's and Dangerfield's deaths both occurred in 1859. Their passings culminated in a kind of watershed moment. Virginia's pro-slavery agenda was roundly and thoroughly disregarded by Fox, whose enormous estate quickly became a refuge for displaced Blacks in Farquier, Orange, and Culpeper counties. And news of John Brown's raid was smoldering throughout the states, ejecting sparks that would inflame abolitionists and radicalize fearful, paranoid slave holders eager to nurture those sparks into the flames of a civil war.

John Fox's family had sent emissaries to all those enslaved by Fox who had taken the offer to migrate to free Ohio while John was still alive, or who had been gifted to family friends as children (as Ailsie had been to Henry Newby). But it would take nearly five years before the news of both her firstborn's death, as well as her fractional inheritance of the Fox estate, would reach Ailsie in Bridgeport. In that time, Dolly Ferguson's heirs had shored up their claims and were steeling themselves to fight a growing number of former slaves, illegitimate heirs, and freed Blacks who had established the Fox estate as their home and were traveling from near and far to stake their claim.

When the chaos around the war had finally died down enough for a hearing to be arranged in regard to the Fox estate, Dolly's heirs would argue that emancipation for all the Fox slaves was unacceptable, as they believed some of those men, women, and children rightfully belonged to them.

John Fox had clearly freed and left his estate to all of the workers his family had enslaved. His will was unambiguous in its directives, but Dolly's heirs fought fiercely to maintain some sliver of the estate for themselves.

I wonder how the Fergusons were able to act without empathy toward those who were born and raised on the grounds. Men, women, and children who perhaps called John Fox their father, who likely cared for him in his sick bed, who ran his businesses and collected his money while the light behind his eyes faded and dulled, were utterly disregarded by Dolly's heirs. I wonder what stories their descendants tell now, and if the jagged edges of greed and impiety have been buffed smooth through retellings.

When Ailsie received Eli Tackett in Bridgeport, she learned that her son was killed at the raid on Harpers Ferry and that his beloved wife and children had been sold down the Ohio River shortly thereafter. She learned that after her departure from the estate, Fox's empire continued to grow exponentially, and was eventually run by all of the mixed-race children Fox had fathered. She learned that the Ferguson heirs would rather scorch the earth the estate stood on than see it fall into the hands of the people who worked within it, people whom they saw as nothing more than property.

I imagine Ailsie and Eli talking long into the night, about the nature of war, the frailty of life, winters in Culpeper and springs in Fauquier. They likely talked about the divine, and they probably talked about love, about how much the children had grown and how brilliant and hardworking they'd all become.

At least, that's what I think they talked about. That's what I hope they talked about.

Following the visit from Eli, Ailsie would return once more to Culpeper, as both a free Ohioan and emancipated Virginian, to not only mourn her firstborn son but to claim a birthright unheard of in pro-slave communities. She was going back to inherit a chunk of the largest, most productive estate in all of Virginia.

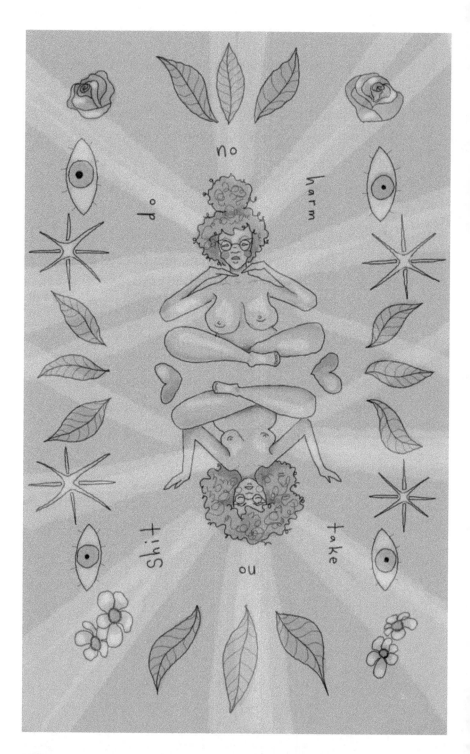

Death

A year had passed since I last spoke to my sister, my cousin, or my aunt. A group text that pinged occasionally and a well-attended email thread would keep me up to date on the developments of the lawsuit, but that was the extent of our communication.

The therapist that cost half of what the lawyer charged told me I should redirect my energy away from the state of my grandmother's house and back to my own life here in Portland. I'd always been independent, so any money I was set to inherit had always felt imaginary. I hadn't spent my life waiting for a payout, so it was a waste of my energy, my therapist said, to obsess over dead rose bushes and dusty pianos a thousand miles away.

That advice felt like a revelation. It felt like permission to not really care too much one way or the other how this whole affair shook out.

After the appointment I thought back to leaving my grandmother's house for what I felt would probably be the last time for a long time. I thought about the wall of photo albums, a row of bookshelves that towered beside a picture window in the sunroom. Albums that would be lost to time. Pictures of my sister in the black satin prom dress I made for her after I first learned to sew. Snapshots of our mother as a teenager, smiling in her paint-splattered denim overalls. Faded images of Fourth of July cookouts and retirement parties. My cousin and I hugging tightly, our smiles mirroring each other. Her holding me as a baby, looking down into my face with the softest, purest love. How long until they too were in boxes, gathering dust and growing mold, stacked atop a beloved parlor piano in the garage?

I thought of them, and looked back at the untouched stack of research I absconded with after my grandmother's funeral.

Who was I to resent anyone?

****

My writing career was stalled. Within weeks of the lawsuit arriving, the website I wrote cannabis reviews for had lost a round of funding and consequently shuttered their Oregon operations, sacking their area team and leaving me without a steady income. I was too exhausted to focus on finding consistent new work, so I limped between meager blog-writing gigs, reapplied for food stamps, and scratched away at the few thousand dollars in savings I'd accrued.

During that year, the case would go to court and a judge would send it to arbitration. While we waited for the trial, the first of the pandemic quarantines rolled up the West Coast. Dates were scheduled and rescheduled while lawyers rearranged Zoom meetings and courtroom visits. We all sat in houses with the rest of our social class. My husband, who worked as a laborer, never missed a day.

It was while we waited for the trial to go to arbitration that George Floyd was murdered.

We were seeing something happening around us, a sharp delineation between ideologies too cacophonous for the spoiled middle class to ignore, regardless of race. The forces that separated Dangerfield from Harriet were still separating fathers from their families. The forces that fought against each other at Harpers Ferry were still fighting. The same forces that left Dangerfield in the street to rot were still murdering Black kids in the street. Not even a pandemic could keep Black blood from spilling at the hands of ignorance, fear, and bigotry.

In the wake of Floyd's murder, Portland raged with protests. Screams and shots and clouds of tear gas shattered the clear blue summer sky of my neighborhood. The lush green of the park blocks on the end of my street glittered with broken glass. Technicolor roses on every curbside perfumed the air, their petals scattered across the pavement like splatters of blood. Death was everywhere.

As the mob overtook Harpers Ferry, empowered by only the color of their skin, did they feel the repetition of history reverberate through them, as I felt it reverberate through me night after night of flash bangs and screaming sirens and hazy trails of pepper spray? Did they recognize the subtle echo of the American promise, that a white person, or a person who wields power, may enact violence to maintain their status quo? The parallels are too brazen to ignore, too all-consuming for complacency.

Are my ancestors watching in horror or resignation?

When my family's case finally arrived in arbitration, a legal arrangement was made between my uncle and aunt. His shares were bought out at the expense of hers, and on the sidelines, my cousin and sister made a handshake deal to share the house. Altogether, it was agreement that was at best a compromise, and at worst a new source of resentment. Either way, it didn't feel like what my grandmother intended.

For weeks, sirens rang out through the night. My depression calcified into dissociation. When my brain grew quiet, strange fruit would begin to crowd my thoughts, which were already a decimated flower garden. My mother, my grandmother, my people and my ancestors' blood running in the street; everyone's roots were exposed, and it was too bright and too loud to not be overwhelmed by.

My grandmother once whispered that "Dangerfield's Body" would have made a better marching song than "John Brown's Body," and when I closed my eyes I could see Dangerfield lying cold in the street, poked at, mutilated, wild pigs eating the flesh of his face as he rotted under the October sky. John Brown's gravesite is a memorial. The alley where Dangerfield was murdered is nicknamed Hog Alley after the merciless way he was left to be devoured. I could see his flesh falling from his face, a face that looked too much like mine to be anything other than half Black and half white.

I stopped closing my eyes. If it wasn't Dangerfield I saw, it was Breonna Taylor, murdered in her sleep; it was Michael Brown, murdered on his knees and left in the August sun to simmer; it was Tamir Rice, a child murdered while at play. These murders were not performed by the kind of pitchfork-wielding vigilantes that stormed Harpers Ferry for a chance to steal Black flesh for a souvenir. These were murders performed by police officers, by men meant to maintain order, enforce laws, protect children.

Am I Black enough to be murdered the same way? Am I white enough to be worthy of security? I don't want to know. I just want to hide.

Instead of joining the protests, I hunched over my desk in the corner of my kitchen and watched video after video. I rewatched the drag queen Tandi Iman Dupree fall from a ceiling into a split during a talent show at least a dozen times. I watched highlights from Miss Continental pageants, I watched NSFW highlights from *Family Feud*, I watched clip packages of reality shows that had aged poorly, and I watched Trixie Mattel unbox her vintage Peaches 'n Cream Barbie.

In a rush, the memory of my grandmother giving me the Black Peaches 'n Cream doll came back to me. Remembering the sharp sting of inadequacy when I realized I'd hurt my grandmother cut through the resentment I'd been building in one swoop.

All the energy I'd poured into my enmity burst loose; a once-focused current now twitched and sparked through me without direction. It compelled me to finally open and truly study Grandma's collection of books and notebooks and journals. This was the legacy. Not the house, not the flower garden, not the piano.

I began to transcribe Ailsie's story, to pull apart the disparate news articles and book chapters and handwritten letters between distant cousins that my grandmother had spent so many of her years assembling into the true inheritance before me.

Protests in parks, marches down avenues, and passionate riots raged in the streets of Portland. Online I posted paintings my mother had left behind, generations of Blackness, kings, queens, families, dressed in gold. I asked the internet how many pieces of Black art existed in their homes. I asked them how much Black lives mattered to them if they weren't celebrating those lives inside the walls where they safely slept.

The neighborhood outside grew louder, so I dove deeper. I was swimming in wealth, I was connected to all my mothers, I was receiving all the lessons I thought I'd missed, I was using all the talents I received: wonder, empathy, honor, legacy, love. The more I untangled, the closer I felt to my mother and grandmother, the closer I felt to feeling purpose.

The first essay I wrote about Dangerfield was published six months later. I began writing for a local newspaper shortly after, a prestigious position I'd coveted for years: writing the cannabis column for Portland's alt-weekly. I wrote it through the lens of Blackness, reminding readers at every opportunity what the Black community sacrificed for cannabis legalization, how the war on drugs, to this day, devastates communities of color, how agriculture is our heritage, and how we can advocate for equity over equality every day.

For the first time since childhood, I felt like I had made my mother and grandmother proud.

To reward myself, I decided to buy both the Black and white versions of the Peaches 'n Cream Barbie that had been the source of so much cultural confusion in my youth. Down the rabbit hole of Barbie dolls, I found not only both the Peaches 'n Cream dolls that had been beautifully reissued, but a brand new variety of Barbie as well.

This new Barbie had strong, thick thighs that tapered into delicate ankles. She wore oversized sneakers and a neon fanny pack. Her skin was a yellowy beige, the distinct gold of racial ambiguity. Her crown was thick with pale blue curls that may have laid flat, but likely only after a great deal of persuasion. Her nose was both wide enough to speak to an African heritage and narrow enough to pass for something altogether different, which, by all accounts, she was. She is. Which by all accounts, I am as well.

I raced to my nearest Target to buy her. When I got to the counter, the cashier looked at the doll, then looked at me and said, "Hey, this doll looks just like you."

My eyes welled with euphoric tears. "I know, right?" I said through my smile.

Resolution

Ailsie's husband and Dangerfield's father Henry died in the summer of 1861, a few months after the start of the Civil War, two years after Dangerfield was murdered at the raid on Harpers Ferry, and three years before Eli Tackett arrived bearing news of John Fox's estate.

By the time of Henry's death, he and Ailsie had been settled in Bridgeport, Ohio for 20 years, and living as spouses for 40 years. When I think about the time they spent tucked in the evangelical cradle of uppercutter country (where even a slave society couldn't uphold a plantocracy, for the topography was too unforgiving to support wealth), I hope they really felt true love, just like my grandma professed them to. I hope that as Ailsie grew older, and bore more of his children, their age gap narrowed. I hope as she aged, a mutual respect blossomed between them and Ailsie felt a genuine desire for the husband to whom she'd been given as a gift. Or maybe it was there all along.

When they first crossed the Virginia/Ohio border during their migration, Henry presented paperwork from John Fox that granted him control of Ailsie, but not outright ownership. This is exceptional, because Henry is recorded as crossing the Ohio River into Bridgeport with his wife, an enslaved negro who, upon placing her feet on the shores of the river, breathed free for the first time in her life.

When I think of Ailsie placing her feet on Ohioan soil, I compulsively take a breath so big it makes me dizzy. It fills my belly, pushes against my solar plexus and threatens to burst through my windpipe. I feel it in my ears and behind my eyes, I feel it in the flush of red that creeps into cheeks and lips. And when I let it out, I feel new.

Henry would perform this migration from the pro-slave Virginia to the free state of Ohio several more times, each journey ending with the freedom of one or two of his children and members of those children's families, until the Newbys all but vanished from Culpeper entirely.

My ancestor Henry Newby was, on paper, a typical slave owner, and fathering and repudiating biracial slaves even posthumously was, by all accounts, normal slave-owner behavior. But Henry freed all of his children, and as many of their children as he could before his death.

His firstborn son, Dangerfield, became a hero of American history. Against impossible odds, Dangerfield gave his life for a cause his father must have known was worth dying for: the freedom of our family, of all families. Henry and Dangerfield both took action against bondage to free the families that they loved. Henry was a success, but that's not to say that Dangerfield was a failure.

History will remember John Brown as a hero of a certain cloth, and Dangerfield as his first raider to perish, but there is a great tapestry of valiance woven by those who sought to upend a detestable structure by not destruction alone, but by searching, sojourning, and building something altogether different.

In his last will and testament, Henry Newby left his entire estate to his wife and mother of his 11 children. Dangerfield's savings, the money he intended for Harriet's freedom, was passed along in the same manner to Ailsie and her remaining children.

****

Eli Tackett had been the Fox estate's miller and groundskeeper. When John Fox's health declined, Eli took on the daily affairs as de facto superintendent. He supervised Fox's lands over the ridge in Shenandoah, walking the distance between acreages in what might have felt like an illusion of freedom; he was seemingly unencumbered by his bondage.

John Fox planned to relocate his slaves to freedom while he lived, but Eli had refused the offer. Manumission was one of the main directives of John Fox's will, which incidentally, was written three years before the issuing of the Emancipation Proclamation.

Though he refused his own manumission, Eli committed himself to John's intention to pass his lands over to his rightful heirs: he would make sure that the slaves who rejected the offer of relocation and instead remained duly dedicated to the Fox estate would inherit these lands.

Dolly Ferguson's children had been raised in waiting for John Fox's death; it was the day they would lay claim to the Fox estate. Eli Tackett knew this, and so he began quietly organizing his master's affairs in preparation, part of which meant sending word to all of John Fox's inheritors, including Ailsie and each of her surviving children.

****

The Newby family had lived most of their lives either on the Newby farm in uppercutter country or in Bridgeport, unaware that they could potentially be legal property of John Fox. Perhaps John Fox himself was unaware, having essentially gifted Ailsie to Henry as a child bride; all the children born from their union were assumed to be property of their father, Henry, an assumption Henry would use to free each of them over the course of his long migration.

But the news of John Fox's passing brought the cold reminder of Ailsie's association with the estate, and that even in freedom, she could be seen in the eyes of the law as something rather than someone. Dolly Ferguson's children were expressly suing the estate for the rights to slaves they believed belonged to them, and thus were ineligible for emancipation, despite manumission being one of the main directives of John Fox's will.

After her meeting with Eli Tackett, Aislie traveled with her daughter Elmira, the same Elmira Dangerfield and Harriet had named their daughter after, back to Culpeper to claim her estate.

There is so much to process in learning about Ailsie's journey from Virginia to Ohio and back again. I wonder if these journeys were fraught, as one might imagine for a freed negro through pro-slavery territories. Or did Ailsie and Elmira travel something more in line with the inferior privilege I'm familiar with, a mixed race identity, with an ability to easily pass?

Ailsie had the newly acquired prerogative of a land-owner. She was free, her children were free, and though her husband had passed, Ailsie Newby traveled with impunity. She returned to her birthplace to claim her rightful share of Virginia's largest estate many times before the estate was finally settled. Every time I visualize that journey it ends with that same, heaving breath that leaves me dizzy but quietly thrilled.

Ailsie left the Fox estate as a child, but, I wonder, had she ever returned? In her younger years, had she ever traveled from the inhospitable terrain of her uppercutter homestead back to trade stories, or just sit and visit over cups of tea and leftover pastries? Did John Fox know her as a mother, or as a grandmother?

I wonder if anyone wrote down the stories they told each other.

I like to imagine Ailsie and her Elmira arriving at the Fox estate and into the arms of the family members they'd left behind. Cousins, aunties, childhood best friends, all these and more had converged upon the Fox estate. Displaced, newly freed persons were welcomed there, to the enormous displeasure of the Fergusons, who would argue this as a blight on their beloved estate, but I dream of something utopian. In the fog of war, surrounded by adversaries, the Fox estate might have been an oasis. A place where Blackness was celebrated, where love could sow seeds, and where freedom was utterly possible, not only within the estate's gilded confines, but beyond.

Ailsie and Elmira would travel back and forth from Bridgeport to Culpeper many times during the mid-1860s, appearing before courts to claim their rights to the estate, only to be rebuffed or rescheduled. The scattered recordings of the complicated proceedings are expired breadcrumbs I've no desire to reassemble into logical pathways. But I know that several years would pass before a manifold judgment was decided; all of Ailsie's children were indeed found to be the erstwhile property of John Fox, and thus the true inheritors to his estate. Dolly Ferguson's children, after years in court, were once again refused access to the vast Fox fortune.

****

I think Ailsie had many reasons to revisit Virginia. More than arguing over her former master's embattled estate, that land was as much her ancestral home as San Pedro is mine. Virginia soil absorbed her son's spilled blood when he challenged its inequities. San Pedro concrete reflected my mother's fallible strength. Virginia sunshine dried Harriet's tears as she held her children, Ailsie's grandchildren, and floated down a river to an unknown fate. San Pedro sunrises browned the back of my uncle's neck as he tended my grandmother's roses. Virginia wildflowers decorated Ailsie's hair as she played on the waterfront with her brothers, sisters, and cousins; maybe they decorated her bedside as well. San Pedro saltwater perfumed my classrooms; tidal discoveries adorned my headboard. Virginia rain nourished the crops Ailsie planted with the husband who vowed her freedom was in reach, and that he would guide her there safely. San Pedro summers brought the man I would marry from his home on the East Coast to the Wild West, and opportunities to thrive in a new way took him and me to territories we too found more serene.

Ailsie returned to Virginia to mourn her son and claim her estate. I returned to San Pedro to wonder what entitles anyone to anything. Even as I stare at the threads of this ancestry – frayed, threadbare, and piecemeal – I wonder how I'm entitled to even run my fingers through them. Even as I write their words, I'm withered by my own audacity to do so.

But who else will?

Afterword

In my grandmother's binders are a half-dozen or so letters to and from a cousin back east named Sherrie. Some of the letters are handwritten, others are printed out threads of late-'90s/early-aughts AOL emails with text ads in the headers and footers but no return email address. There are pages and pages of typed notes that I suspected were sent to or dictated by my grandmother.

Cousin Sherrie was a primary contact for my grandmother's research, and as I sift through the ephemera of family pictures and shared new cutouts, I see that Sherrie and my grandmother were working in tandem to uncover more and more of our shared history. They wrote to each other in a tender way, like two cousins separated in youth and reunited in adulthood; they were constantly catching each other up on the news of each other's families. Some of Sherrie's letters are too old to be legible, the lead of the pencil with which they were written long dissolved into crispy old notebook paper that has begun to mold around the edges.

In organizing the stories of Ailsie, Henry, and Dangerfield, it was both my grandmother and our cousin Sherrie's work whom I referenced. Though my heart only really recognized my grandmother's work, Sherrie's was also exhaustive. Her own retelling of our family history was a chapter in the binders that I referenced again and again without really acknowledging that it was this cousin's work, rather my grandmother's. I remember her name coming up often as my grandmother's work gathered steam, but I do not remember her. I don't think we've ever met.

The year before my grandmother passed, a book detailing the lives of the five Black men in John Brown's army was published. Written by Eugene Meyer, *Five For Freedom: The African-American Soldiers in John Brown's Army* features Dangerfield prominently. It wasn't until well after I'd strung together Ailsie's story using my grandmother's piecemeal collection, about four years after her funeral, that this new book found its way into my personal library. In the first chapter of this book, around 25 pages in, the author references a source. A woman named Sherrie Carter.

Cousin Sherrie.

Encountering her name in this historical account of the raid on Harpers Ferry sent church bells ringing in my head. I saw her name there in print, and in a rush, remembered how many times I had seen the name Sherrie scrawled in either my grandmother's dramatic script or as a squat, rounded signature usually following a letter written in pencil. The letters between them were personal, and reading them felt a bit intrusive, so I primarily stuck to the clippings and references they assembled, and avoided the post-mortems they shared with each other.

Cousin Sherrie's catalog was far more expansive than my grandmother's binders had led me to believe. When *Five for Freedom* was being written, Sherrie supplied this author with her vast collection of historical research, some of which she'd inherited from the author of *Migrants Against Slavery*. Tucked into the bibliography for *Migrants Against Slavery*, Philip Schwartz notes he "is indebted to Sherrie Carter." I wonder if my grandmother ever came up in conversation.

For every fifth thing I learn in the pages of these books and binders, there's a bit that lived only between my grandmother and me, or whoever was in the room when she was sharing stories. The binders make no note of Dangerfield being the prototype for a Quentin Tarantino movie protagonist, but Grandma grousing about Dangerfield being the real Django was family lore.

But, I suppose, Dangerfield and Django and many other black ancestry conflations are lore for far more Black families than I'll ever grasp. For us, Dangerfield was a hero, an idol, and we should all aspire to be as brave, as brilliant, as resilient, and as devoted as the immortal Dangerfield. Of course someone would commodify his story, or a story just like his. It was up to us to tell it right. She was building him the legacy he deserved, the recognition he deserved. She was grasping at threads, just like I am now.

No, no...she wasn't grasping. She was braiding. She was knitting. She was cultivating, and now I was seeing the fruit of those labors. I was tending her roses.

Grandma was gone. Here in the present, I get to see Dangerfield celebrated and examined and glorified. Either in essays I write, or in deeply researched tomes that center him and the other Black raiders, or in museum exhibits telling the story of the Civil War, like the one my publisher saw right after he asked to publish this book.

Around the same time I received the book *Five for Freedom*, my uncle's case had been settled and my aunt and cousin had begun the process of taking out a mortgage in order to buy my share of the estate. The outcome of the case was gratuitous. My uncle would receive only slightly more than he was initially set to inherit, my aunt sacrificing a share of her inheritance to meet his demands and purge him from the trust. Considering costs, I estimate my uncle probably came out with quite a bit less than he would have had he not sued us in the first place.

The liquid assets of the trust, i.e. the cash, was exhausted in order to buy my uncle's share of the house as quickly and painlessly as possible. I'd long since relaxed into the reality that it could be several months, or even a year before I felt I'd received an inheritance commensurate with what I'd felt my cousin and sister had already received.

It was spring of 2021 when the dust from the case settled, and we were all traveling to Las Vegas for another family member's wedding. It would be the first time all of us, the sisters, cousins, and aunties of the estate, were seeing each other since Christmas more than a year prior. And, somehow, when we all saw each other for the first time, there was no time or love lost.

Over dinner, my aunt described me as a perfect angel in regards to how little I outwardly stressed about my monetary inheritance. Without thinking about it too much, I smiled and agreed. My sister had vacillated back and forth between wanting to stay in the house indefinitely, wanting to sell the house, and wanting to take an immediate buyout to be paid out at her discretion, and the vague language of the trust justified her. Arguing with her felt like being stuck in a house of mirrors; besides, it was established, I had my own business to mind. When the paperwork fell into place later that year, I would inherit the equivalent of my grandmother's life savings.

Now was the time to earn it.

Driving home from the wedding, away from the ashy brown desert and into the evergreen mist of the Northwest, I wept for sisterhoods lost at the deaths of mothers and grandmothers; I wept for the self that felt inadequate, resentful, grasping and thrashing when a lifeline had been there the whole time.

With every page of this memoir, the white-hot enmity I'd felt towards my family and the events of the past few years was burning down to ashes and embers. I'd still not been back to visit San Pedro, but I was no longer harboring all the animosity that had kept me, physically at least, out of my family's lives for the past couple of years.

In the early 2010s, my cousin had traveled with our grandmother to a family reunion in Ohio. She was our grandmother's concierge, but also seemed genuinely engrossed in all the history she was able to absorb throughout the course of their trip.

More than a decade later, after reading Sherrie Carter's name in *Five for Freedom*, I reached out to my cousin.

"Oh, that's Cuz'n Sherrie!" she exclaimed as I described the book and its contents.

I had yet to admit to her that I had recently written my own memoir, but her exclamation was so authentic, I heard the same effervescence in her voice that I heard so many years ago when she and Grandma described the adventures they had on their trip. I couldn't contain myself.

She squealed when I told her about my memoir. "Oh Cousin, I'm so proud of you, sometimes it feels like I birthed you myself." When I told her that I wasn't exactly kind, that the story I was telling didn't exactly spotlight the best in us, she drew in a sharp breath and said, "Cousin, I love you, and if I ever said anything that hurt you, you just have to know how sorry I am."

Later that week I reached out to my sister and told her the same thing. She laughed and said, "I love it. Drag us. We absolutely deserve it. "

While on the phone with my cousin, I asked if she still had Grandma's address book, a 40-year-old, raggedy notebook with half its pages fluttering dangerously on a single scrap that connected them to a rusty spiral. Thousands of contacts meticulously noted over decades in the same exact script. She said, *of course she still had the address book*. She is, of course, a keeper of all things. I asked her to send me Sherrie's contact information and told her, in an offhand way that surprised me, that I wanted to pick up where Grandma left off.

After we said our goodbyes and hung up the phone, I sat at my desk, all of Grandma's binders spread out before me. The crowded table was chaotic with pictures, my sketchbooks, history books already published, Sherrie's letters, Grandma's clippings. I looked at everything, and for the first time in my entire life, knew unequivocally that I had done something to make my ancestors proud.

I was no longer drowning in self pity, greed, and resentment. I was swimming in relief.

Acknowledgements

Altogether Different would not have been possible if not for Sherrie Carter, aka Cousin Sherrie. Sherrie's research into Newby family history was more than primary resource; her works have provided creative inspiration, an ancestral conduit, and a vital reconnection with my grandmother, whose relationship and correspondence with "Cuz'n Sherrie" is the reason this book exists. Thank you Sherrie, you will always have my utmost gratitude and reverence.

I'm also deeply grateful to my partner, Craig Flipy whose support was vital to this books completion. I also thank all my various mentors: Joshua James Amberson for holding my hand through the first draft of this manuscript, Suzette Smith for fortifying my foundation and encouraging its growth, Kate Ryan for refining my critiques and sharpening my voice, and Willamette Week for amplifying, celebrating, and standing behind my work.

Thank you to Michael Schepps and Molly Simas at Korza Books for not only facilitating this memoir, but also making it so much better in the process. Thank you to both my RuCrew and Quadrafecta squads for being exceptionally supportive homies through and through.

Thank you to my family, I'm only exploiting our drama in the hopes it helps other families navigate their own. And finally, thank you to my mother and grandmother may they both rest in peace.

Works Cited

Chapter One: San Pedro

Page 15: "The majority of those Black residents were displaced without adequate recompense, the city citing eminent domain..."

"Displacement in North and Northeast Portland – An Historical Overview." Portland Housing Bureau. Accessed April 9, 2023. https://www.portlandoregon.gov/phb/article/655460

Page 29: ""History is not the past. It is the present.... We are our history...the world is not white; it never was white, cannot be white. White is a metaphor for power."

Baldwin, James; Peck, Raoul, dir. 2016. *I Am Not Your Negro*. Velvet Film.

Page 30: ""And there has never been any genuine confrontation between those two levels of experience"

James Baldwin quoted in Peck, Raoul *I Am Not Your Negro: Companion Edition*. (New York: Vintage Books, 2017) p.99-101

Chapter Two: Culpeper

Page 33: "A little more than 150 miles east of Culpeper is Point Comfort, where in 1619, a ship carrying 20 enslaved Africans arrived on the colony's shore, heralding the start of the North Atlantic slave trade"

Jones, Nikole H., Jazmine Hughes, Jake Silverstein, New York Times Magazine, and Smithsonian Institute. 2019. "The 1619 Project." *The New York Times Magazine* (New York), August 18, 2019, 9-10.

Page 35: "His estate was substantial, and, in regards to slave labor, productive"

Carter, Sherrie. *Who We Are: A Story of Strong and Lasting Roots of Black Fauquier County.* Self-published manuscript, 2001 edition. Typescript, p2.

Page 35: "When Sam Fox died in 1804, he left his entire estate, including 16 enslaved men, women, and children, to his own scions, James, John, and Elizabeth Fox-Blackwell"

"Samuel Fox Inventory" reproduced in Carter, p.3. (2001 Edition).

Page 35: "Her name was Dolly Ferguson"

Carter, p. 10-11 (2001 Edition).

Page 37: "The Fox chattel of enslaved persons was then passed down again to the youngest Fox heir, John."

Carter, p 2. (2001 Edition).

Page 38: "He was perceived as a stocky, morose bachelor who kept to himself, but perhaps what his neighbors saw was not the same as what the slaves he fathered saw."

Carter, p.10 (2001 Edition)

Page 38: "...Eli Tackett, an enslaved Black man, who, in John Fox's records, is listed as 'Mulatto'"

"'Census Records' reproduced in Carter, p.12-13. (2001 Edition).

Page 39: "a sympathetic slavemaster..."

"Sarah or Sallie Bywaters' Account" Reproduced in Carter, Sherrie. *Who We Are: A Story of Strong and Lasting Roots of Black Fauquier County.* Self-published manuscript, 2004 edition. Typescript, p6.

Page 40: "Ailsie worked exclusively in the main house of the Fox Estate, a job primarily reserved for the light-skinned enslaved."

Carter, p.6 (2001 Edition)

Chapter Four: Agency

Page 54: "...the endless trade of human chattel between plantations."

"Sarah or Sallie Bywaters' Account" Reproduced in Carter, p6. (2004 Edition)

Chapter 6: Dangerfield

Page 100: "....the first of John Brown's raiders to die during the raid on Harpers Ferry"

Schwarz, Phillip, *Migrants Against Slavery: Virginians and the Nation* (Virginia: University Press of Virginia 2001), p 149.

Page 102: "...seven years later, more than 150 people were killed and Confederates burned at least a quarter of the town."

Stanley, Matthew "First Sack of Lawrence," *Civil War on the Western Border: The Missouri- Kansas Conflict, 1854-1856* The Kansas City Public Library, Accessed June 6, 2023 at https://civilwaronthewesternborder.org/encyclopedia/first-sack-lawrence

Page 102: "John Brown, who had relocated from New York to Kansas with five of his twenty children to fight pro-slavery forces..."

"John Brown". Kansas Historical Society. Created December 1969, Modified November 2021 Archived from the original on April 6, 2022 at https://web.archive.org/web/20220406234901/https://www.kshs.org/kansapedia/john-brown/11731

Page 103: "There will be no peace in this land until slavery is done for..."

Villard, Oswald *John Brown 1800-1859: A Biography 50 Years After* (United Kingdom: Houghton Mifflin, 1910) P.248

Page 104: ""Rough, unsightly."

Anderson, Osborne Perry. *A Voice From Harper's Ferry: A Narrative of Events at Harper's Ferry, With Incidents Prior and Subsequent to its Capture by Captain Brown and His Men* (Boston, 1816, Printed for the Author, Library of Congress Reprint Edition 2022) P.7.

Page 106: "I b'leve I'll go wid de ole man.'"

Douglass, Frederick *The Life and Times of Frederick Douglass*, (1881, reprint New York: Pathway Press, 1941), pp 390-391

Page 106: "he's said to have been dedicated to the railroad's support"

Meyer, Eugene, *Five For Freedom: The African American Soldiers in John Brown's Army* (Chicago: Chicago Review Press, 2018), p 22.

Page 106: "working as a blacksmith for Edwards' brother, that he met John Brown"

Meyer, p 23.

Page 106: "We aren't buying men."

Meyer, p.23

Page 109: "And between all that, they were rented out to work on farms around the counties"

Schwarz, p.159.

Page 111: "Between 1826 and 1844 Ailsie Newby gave birth to ten more children,"
Carter, p.17 (2004 Edition)

Page 111: "she was known in their small foothill community as Henry's wife"
Schwarz, p.151

Page 112: "had a reputation as a canny and vigorous young worker"
Schwarz, pp. 159-160

Page 115: "P.S. write soon if you please"
Newby, Harriet to Newby, Dangerfield, unknown, 2009 in *African American trailblazers in American History* - Library of Virginia Publications and Educational Services. Originally at www.lva.virginia.gov/public/trailblazers/res/Harriet_Newby_Letters.pdf mirrored on https://pdfsecret.com/download/letters-from-harriet-newby-library-of-virginia_5a304cb6d64ab21cdb5f30fc_pdf accessed June 8, 2023
From the original:
Governor's Message and Reports of the Public Officers of the State, of the Boards of Directors, and of the Visitors, Superintendents, and Other Agents of Public Instruction or Interests of Virginia (Richmond, 1859), 116-117. Special Collections, Library of Virginia, Richmond, Virginia.

Page 116: "increase the price after Dangerfield had presented the payment in full"
  Schwarz, p.162

Page 116: *P s write soon*
  Newby, Harriet to Newby, Dangerfield, unknown, Special Collections, Library of Virginia, Richmond, Virginia.

Page 119: ""a smart and good man for an ignorant one.""
  Laughlin-Schultz, Bonnie. "Annie Brown, Soldier," *The Tie That Bound Us: The Women of John Brown's Family and The Legacy of Radical Abolitionism*, (New York: Cornell University Press, 2013).

Page 119: "a quiet man who never talked much about slavery and kept his intentions for joining John Brown to himself"
  Schwarz, p.160

Chapter 8: The Raid

Page 131:"She called them her "invisibles."
  Laughlin-Schultz, p. 54.

Page 132:" It was there in Chatham that Anderson reportedly first met John Brown and learned of his plan to raid Harpers Ferry"

Calarco, Tom *People of the Underground Railroad: A Biographical Dictionary* (Connecticut: Greenwood Publishing Group, 2008), p.255.

Page 133: "dullness growing out of restraint by their kindness."

Anderson, P.25 (Library of Congress Reprint Edition 2022).

Page 134: "One hung themselves after learning they would be sold south"

Anderson, p. 20 (Library of Congress Reprint Edition 2022).

Page 135: "Osborne Perry Anderson describes Dangerfield as his comrade,"

Anderson, p. 40 (Library of Congress Reprint Edition 2022).

Page 135: "John Brown rose earlier than usual and called his men down from their bunks to pray."

Anderson, p. 28 (Library of Congress Reprint Edition 2022).

Page 136: ""You can have my slaves, if you will let me remain."

Anderson, p.34 (Library of Congress Reprint Edition 2022).

Page 136: "He blubbered"
        Anderson, p.34 (Library of Congress Reprint
Edition 2022).

Page 137: "But if it was necessary, then to make sure work
of it."
        Anderson, p.29 (Library of Congress Reprint
Edition 2022).

Page 138: "if the citizens interfere with me I must only
burn the town and have blood."
        Meyer, p.86

Page 141: "THE INSURRECTIONISTS SAY THEY HAVE
COME TO FREE THE SLAVES AND INTEND TO DO IT
AT ALL HAZARDS"
        Transcribed from the *New York Daily Tribune,*
October 18, 1859 quoted in Kent, Zachary, *Cornerstones of
Freedom; The Story of John Brown's Raid on Harpers Ferry.*
(Chicago: Children's Press, 1988), p.17.

Page 141: ""Kill Them! Kill Them!"
        Meyer, p.90

Page 141: "Dangerfield had been stationed at the
Shenandoah Bridge."
        Meyer, p.90

Page 142: "Stealing his flesh for souvenirs."
        Meyer, pp.90-91

Pages 143: Harriet Newby Letter
Newby, Harriet to Newby, Dangerfield, unknown, Special Collections, Library of Virginia, Richmond, Virginia.

Page 145: "And they never came."
Meyer, p.79

Page 145: "A splendid light skinned specimen"
Laughlin-Schultz, p.60

Chapter 10: Reintroduction

Page 161: "Fox's estate, as was his wish, was to be dispersed to all those he enslaved."
"John Fox Last Will and Testament" reproduced in Carter, Sherrie. *Who We Are: A Story of Strong and Lasting Roots of Black Fauquier County.* Self-published manuscript, 2001 edition. Typescript, pp. 10-11.

Page 162: "14-year-old Elmira (or "Mira" as she was nicknamed) was left in Virginia to fend for herself."
Carter, p. 33 (2001 edition)

Page 163: "...he intended to leave the entirety of the Virginia estate to his remaining living slaves"
Cater, pp. 31-32 (2004 edition)

Page 163 "Those that did not wish to migrate should inherit the estate which they had dedicated their lives to"
Meyer, pp. 18-19

Page 164: "they'd already been prepared to fight for a share of the inheritance"
Carter, p.28 (2001 Edition)

Chapter 10: Resolution

Page 180: "Dangerfield's savings, the money he intended for Harriet's freedom, was passed along in the same manner to Ailsie and her remaining children"
Schwarz, pp.164-165

Brianna Wheeler is an award winning essayist and illustrator from San Pedro, California. This is her first memoir

Also From Korza Books

Is It Just Me Or Are We Nailing This? Essays on BoJack Horseman
Published with Antiquated Future
Joshua James Amberson, Timothy Day, Jessica Fonvergne, Lauren Hobson, M.L. Schepps, Jourdain Searles and Molly E. Simas
Illustrations from Eileen Chavez, Ross Jackson, Naomi Marshall and Sarah Shay Mirk

Split Aces
M.L. Schepps

Poetry For People: Fifty Years of Writing
Dixie Lubin

How To Forget Almost Everything
Joshua James Amberson

The Novel Killer (Coming 2024)
Kate Shelton